Swarthmore Lecture 1980

WHAT CANST THOU SAY?

towards a Quaker theology

by Janet Scott

QHS

QUAKER HOME SERVICE · LONDON

First published May 1980

ISBN 0 85245 151 2

Cover design by John Blamires

Printed in Great Britain in 11/12 Times
by Headley Brothers Ltd., The Invicta
Press, Ashford, Kent and London

PREFACE

The Swarthmore Lectureship was established
by the Woodbrooke Extension Committee at a
meeting held December 9th, 1907: the minute
of the Committee providing for 'an annual
lecture on some subject relating to the message
and work of the Society of Friends'. The name
Swarthmore was chosen in memory of the
home of Margaret Fox, which was always open
to the earnest seeker after Truth, and from
which loving words of sympathy and
substantial material help were sent to fellow
workers.

The lectureship has a twofold purpose: first, to
interpret further to the members of the Society
of Friends their message and mission; and,
secondly, to bring before the public the spirit,
the aims and fundamental principles of Friends.
The lecturer alone is responsible for any
opinions expressed.

The lectureship provides both for the publication
of a book and for the delivery of a lecture, the
latter usually at the time of assembly of London
Yearly Meeting of the Society of Friends. A lecture
related to the present book was delivered at
Friends House, Euston Road, London, on
the evening of May 23rd, 1980.

FOREWORD

'What canst thou say?' was only the first of
three questions which George Fox asked and
which Margaret Fell said cut her to the heart
so that she cried bitterly. The other two were
'Art thou a child of Light and hast walked in
the Light?' and 'What thou speakest is it
inwardly from God?'

The close connection of these three with
their demand that what we say be closely
rooted both in spiritual experience and in
moral living, forms the most profound
challenge to the Quaker theologian. For our
theology must involve not only spiritual and
intellectual integrity but also the obedience
that seeks to live the truth.

Anyone therefore who is bold enough to
attempt a Quaker theology must feel
unworthy of the task. Yet this cannot excuse
us from the responsibility to answer the
demand to speak.

In taking up this task I am grateful for the
help and support of many people, not least
my family who have lived with me. I thank,
too, the Friends and colleagues who have
read the drafts and pointed out the graver
errors. Any faults that remain are mine alone.

Most of all I am thankful to all the Friends in
Meetings throughout the world who by their
patient listening to the voice of God and their
ministry in words, silence and action, have
taught me what it means to be a Quaker. If
mine are the words, theirs is the spirit. I hope
that I have reflected it truly.

Janet Scott

CONTENTS

CONTENTS

I

IN THE BEGINNING, GOD

In the silence, waiting, Quakers know God. We feel the presence, sometimes as a gentle comforter, sometimes a firm assurance, sometimes a light that illuminates our thoughts and gives us new words, sometimes a fearful reality whose loving, tender, awful power enters our pounding hearts and trembling bodies.

We know this power, this light, this reality, this tender love, as individuals and at any time, but we know it most surely in our meetings for worship together where, at our best, we help, encourage and guide each other, taking, as it were, the clay of the experience and together moulding it into a new and different form which no one mind, but only the eternal, could have envisaged.

This is the essential truth of Quakerism, held not as a belief but as experience. However, our experience is wider than this and carries with it other discoveries which we must express in words but which we know first as living truth.

We have found that this power, this light, turns us from evil to good and brings us into unity with God and thence with our fellows, into that 'spirit which takes away the occasion of all wars.'[1]

George Fox, writing in his journal in 1648, expresses it as 'Great things did the Lord lead me into, and wonderful depths were opened unto me, beyond what can by words be declared; but as people come into subjection to the spirit of God, and grow up in the image and power of the Almighty, they may receive the Word of wisdom, that opens all things, and come to know the hidden unity in the Eternal Being. . . . And as the Lord opened these things unto me, I felt his power went forth over all, by which all might be reformed, if they would receive and bow unto it.'[2]

And in his Epistle 181 of 1659: 'Live in the unchangeable power of God, which will keep you in righteousness, and truth, and love, and unity ... patiently in the power of the Lord wait, that in it ye may all be kept low, in love and unity with God and one with another.'[3]

We have found also that this Spirit is available to everyone, it speaks to that which is universal in the human heart. There are no pre-conditions of belief or morality. It speaks to us even if we will not listen, but if we do heed, it draws us to itself, however we name it and whether we name it or not. We may be Christian or atheist, Jew or Muslim, Marxist, Buddhist, Hindu—the spirit seeks us, and loves us, and calls us to turn to the universal love and unity.

As George Fox wrote in 1683, 'God, who made all, pours out of his spirit upon all men and women in the world ... yea, upon whites and blacks, Moors, and Turks, and Indians, Christians, Jews and Gentiles, that all with the spirit of God, might know God and the things of God, and serve and worship him in his spirit and truth, that he hath given them.'[4]

And as Isaac Penington wrote: 'Though they had never heard the outward Sound, or Name Christ; yet feeling the thing, and being gathered to God by the thing, the Value and Vertue of it could not but redound to them. For it is not the outward Name, but the inward Life and Power which is the Saviour.'[5]

We know too that God may work through men, women and children; that the stumbling words spoken by a young person may be of more worth than the polished offering of a weighty elder.

Early in our history, James Parnell, aged fifteen, small and frail, walked a hundred and fifty miles, driven to seek George

Fox. 'Little James', 'the Quaking boy', in four short years preached, suffered and was martyred, leaving an undying example of selfless obedience.

Again from our early days we have a letter written from a Friend in Reading: 'Our little children kept the meetings up, when we were all in prison, notwithstanding that wicked justice when he came and found them there ... would pull them out of the Meeting, and punch them in the back till some of them were black in the face.'

Our women have always been partners with our men. The Society grew from both the prophetic ministry of George Fox and the nurture and care of Margaret Fell and her daughters.

Fox wrote: 'I was moved of the Lord to recommend to Friends, for the benefit and advantage of the Church of Christ, that the faithful women who were called to the belief of the Truth, being made partakers of the same precious faith, and heirs of the same everlasting Gospel of life and salvation as the men are, might in like manner come into the possession and practice of the Gospel order ... That so all the family of God, women as well as men, might know, possess, perform, and discharge their offices and services in the house of God.'[6]

Fox knew these 'faithful women' who had worked and suffered for the faith; women like Mary Fisher who travelled to Turkey to speak to the Grand Turk; and the first convert to Quakerism, Elizabeth Hooton, 'a very tender woman' Fox says, who was imprisoned, whipped, placed in the stocks, but travelled in England and America, and finally died in Jamaica, 'though the day before she had been among Friends in the town, exhorting them to be faithful in the works of God.'

So our witness is that the Spirit can bring every person into the life of obedience and love. We witness further, that this is a direct relationship, that though we may all help and minister to each other there is no need of a mediator between ourselves and

God—the Spirit reaches out to each one with no intermediary. There is no need of special times or of special places. Though for convenience we fix times and places to meet each other, the Spirit meets with us at any time and in any place; we cannot fetter the free workings of God. Nor do we need any special ceremony, or objects, no sacrifice, no altar, no bread, wine or water, no candles, incense, music or vestments, no chants, hymns or words, only the turning of a willing heart.

And although we worship in silence and stillness we also know as individuals that God can break into activity and speak through events, that every moment can be lived in the divine presence.

We also testify that what we have experienced cannot be tied down to any one form of words. Though we must try to communicate what we know, our expression always falls short of the reality. We cannot assent to any creed as unalterably true for 'the letter killeth but the Spirit giveth life.'

William Penn put it like this: 'It is not opinion, or speculation, or notions of what is true, or assent to or the subscription of articles and propositions, though never so soundly worded that . . . makes a man a true believer or a true Christian. But it is a conformity of mind and practice to the will of God . . . according to the dictates of this Divine principle of Light and Life in the soul which denotes a person truly a child of God.'[7]

This is the truth which we know and try to live. It is 'a working description of practical religion rather than a systematic theology',[8] but I wish to sum it up as a series of propositions:

1. that every person is capable of response to the divine Spirit;
2. that this Spirit, or Light, or God, reaches out to each one directly and freely;
3. that if we follow the leadings of this Spirit faithfully we are led out of sin, into unity with the divine will;

4

4. that this unity leads us into love of and care for all human-kind, who are our kin;
5. that what the Spirit shows us is living truth which cannot be fettered by words.

II

FACING THE QUESTIONS

I have stated it like this because I think that this is a 'working definition' of Quakerism which is both based on tradition and currently valid. But there is a significant difference in this from what early Friends held.

George Fox based his Quakerism firmly on his experience of the Light Within. But in interpreting his experience, particularly when disputing with other churches, he supported his beliefs by expressing them in terms of his view of Christianity based on his interpretation of the scriptures. He believed that Quakerism was primitive Christianity restored; and Friends wrote many tracts and pamphlets to defend this position.

Thus Fox's belief in the universality of the life within was defended by reference to the pre-existence of the incarnate Christ. He had no separate priesthood, because all were priests under Christ, the Prophet, Priest and King.[9] He had no sacraments because he believed that Christ had already come and he was living in the 'Day of the Lord'. Men and women were equal because they had been restored to the position before the Fall.

However, what Fox and other Friends supported by their definition of Christianity we may now hold as true on other grounds. We may base these propositions not only on our current experience of the spirit (as early Friends did on their experience) but also on our collective experience of more than three hundred years as we have developed ways of responding to the light within and of recognising guidance.

This light or spirit has always been the basis of authority in the Society of Friends. In following it we are made free to look at our origins with a critical eye and to rethink our beliefs.

7

As David Jenkins says, 'I believe that to know God is to be free to question everything. I further believe that to know God is to be bound to question anything.'[10]

If we do then question we see that at the heart of Quaker theology there is an important, indeed a crucial, problem that has never been solved. One might, in fact, surmise that it has only been our reluctance to engage in theology that has prevented us from tearing ourselves apart. This problem is the tension between two basic beliefs, Christianity and Universalism, the belief, on the one hand, that the Inner Light is the Light of Christ, and, on the other hand, that it is in everyone whether or not they have heard of Jesus. The traditional Quaker view, which stressed the Inearnate Word at the expense of the historical Jesus, was not satisfactory in Christian terms in that it did not explain the relationship between the Word and Jesus.[11] Now we must see that it is not satisfactory in Universalist terms. For in the face of long devout religious traditions such as those of the Jews, Muslims, Hindus it is arrogant to maintain that the truth which they know must, and can only, be explained adequately in Christian terms.

Is it then necessary for us to identify the Spirit or Light with the Risen Christ as Fox and the early Friends did? Rachel King writes:

> The theory that has been outlined, the Light as that which shows a man evil and the Light as that in which is unity, does not really take into account the Christian revelation. Fox's central position can be held without reference to historical Christianity. His theory that the universal saving Light within is the only teacher and authority is too general to be specifically Christian. There is no logical need for the incarnation and the passion in Fox's central religious conceptions. When Fox talks about Christ's dying for us and

redeeming us, he is simply using inherited terminology without co-ordinating it with his other thought.[12]

Quakerism had to be Christian in origin, because in seventeenth-century England, the thought-world was such that Christian assumptions were unchallenged. There was no alternative. But is this a permanent connection? What is the relationship between Quakerism and Christianity? What is the relationship between Quakerism and other major faiths? Is it possible to maintain both these relationships?

The question 'Are Quakers Christian?' has occupied much of the Society's attention in recent years. Henry Cadbury gave one answer to it in his Swarthmore Lecture of 1957,[13] which he concluded with an appreciation of the variety in Christianity: 'The true catholicity of Christianity is a precious heritage to the church universal and to its every branch. The over-zealous advocates of conformity have forgotten their scriptures. Their Bible begins with a story of a "good" creation in which it is said that the flora and fauna were made in variety and were each "brought forth after its kind". It ends with a heavenly city approached not by one narrow way and one strait gate, but with several gates facing each quarter of the compass.'

But this question is one with which I shall deal only incidentally for it is only part of the problem. For as we try to answer questions about Quakerism and our relation to Christianity and other faiths, we shall see other problems arise. What is Christianity? What can we now say about Jesus? How do we know when we have the right answers? What in this sort of question counts as knowledge and truth?

In short, we need to start thinking about theology. In his 1965 Swarthmore Lecture,[14] John Macmurray wrote:

Holding fast to our refusal to define our faith in doctrinal terms might we not create a new and acceptable kind of

9

theology, which should be undogmatic, and which, like modern science, would recognise the hypothetical and temporary character of all its findings? Such an effort, as I see it, should proceed under certain presuppositions. It should be empirical in temper, checking theory against contemporary experience, religious and scientific. It should be freely critical of the past, recognising that in this field of knowledge as in others, antiquity is no indication of validity. It should recognise that it is impossible to believe what one does not understand, and undesirable to profess to believe what one cannot believe effectively. It should be concerned to reject openly and explicitly what it can no longer accept, and it should not expect nor too eagerly desire unanimity.

I invite you to join me in taking up this task. It is nothing less than to attempt to achieve a Quaker theology for this generation, one that has room for both a Christian and a Universalist emphasis and that seeks to maintain and express the Quaker propositions we have derived from experience.

III

WHAT CAN WE SAY?

What then is a theology?

Although it attempts to deal with and explain eternal truth, theology is by no means permanent or static. As we look back over the history of Judaism and Christianity we can see that ideas are changed and developed. New problems arise, new influences are brought to bear and the old answers have to be adapted.

The most helpful way to regard theology is as a process, continually ongoing, as we search not only for meaning but to express meaning. So we must be able to accept that any conclusions we reach are only temporary, that what is truth for us is only a stepping stone for the future.

This process should fulfil two major conditions, that it is contemporary and that it is inclusive. It should be contemporary, first, in that it should be concerned with current religion and experience. We live in an age which has lost any facile confidence in human progress. We have seen the darkness in human hearts, in war and holocaust,[15] genocide, terrorism and torture. We know that we can destroy ourselves. We can see religion as one of those factors that separate communities and encourage hatred and conflict. But it is also a time of hope, a crisis time when it becomes clear to us that we must choose and uphold our values. The church is at last repenting of internal conflict and seeking to travel the thorny road to reconciliation. We are learning the value of other faiths and in meeting and knowing Jews, Sikhs, Muslims, Hindus, in seeing their courage and devotion, we are discovering in a much more personal way that we must respect the light given to others and look for unity with them.

We must be especially cheered by those who were formerly exploited who are facing up to power and refusing to be oppressed further: the women who are demanding their full place in the church and society; the low-paid who are making us realise that there is a need for justice; the third world countries who are beginning to see that our technology will not benefit them and who are choosing their own way.

Our theology must speak to, and of, the world we know. As Penington said, 'That through which men are saved is the dispensation of Truth in their Age. The measure of light which God gives forth in every Age; that is the means and proper way of Salvation in that Age.'[16]

We should be contemporary, secondly, in the ways we think. We need to be reasonable and rational, to think clearly and logically. We need to be critical, bold in rejecting what we cannot defend and clear in stating the grounds on which we proceed. We need to take account of current knowledge, of psychology and sociology, of science, philosophy and the study of language; above all of theological and biblical studies. Yet, in doing so, we shall hope to maintain the Quaker principle that these are but aids to understanding the truth, and that what is important is to live in the truth.

We should be contemporary, thirdly, in the problems with which we deal. Each age has significant questions which come to its notice. Thus, we shall not consider the relationship between religion and the state, which greatly occupied early Friends. We shall not expound such matters as baptism, which are for the moment not theologically urgent.

But we shall need to consider the vital questions of this decade, and we shall do this in three areas. We must consider the problem of Jesus and whether and in what way he can be called divine. We must consider the problem which is 'top of the theological agenda', the doctrine of God. And we must bear in

12

mind, even if they are only mentioned briefly, the problems of church unity and inter-faith relationships.

So we aim to be contemporary in our view of the world, in our ways of thinking and in the problems raised.

We should also be inclusive. By this I mean that we must understand religion not just as an intellectual exercise but as something which involves the whole personality. Our attitudes, emotions, behaviour and values are all involved and our thinking must be concerned with them. We cannot separate theology into a separate box that neither draws on our personal experience and ways of life nor contributes to them. This means in particular, that theology should be moral. Our Quaker principles that the light leads out of sin and into unity also imply this. It should be moral towards people. That is, it must take seriously their deepest concerns and try to avoid facile answers. Thus, the problem of suffering has to be taken into account and the values of freedom, justice, equality and concern for others.

Theology must also be concerned with the ethical results of its activities. We may not make on religious grounds a statement we would regard as wrong on moral or social grounds, or encourage cruelty or oppression or hatred. On the contrary, it should give guidance towards the practical ways of living which should result from its conclusions.

It must also be moral towards God. It may not make any statement about God that is unworthy, or that implies that God does not reach our highest moral standards, or that allows God to be used as a justification for immoral action.

Our theology must also be inclusive towards other faiths and towards atheism. That is that it must take them seriously, respect their principles and concerns, and seek to find them a place which justifies and does not condemn them. Thus, although it is impossible for me to speak in other than theist

13

terms and this contradicts atheism, I must not thereby maintain that people are wrong to be atheists.

George Fox wrote:

> Take heed of judging the measures of others, but every one mind your own; and there ye famish the busy minds and high conceits, and so peace springs up among you and division is judged. And this know, that there are diversities of gifts but one spirit, and unity therein to all who with it are guided. And though the way seems to thee diverse; yet judge not the way, lest thou judge the Lord, and knowest not that several ways (seeming to reason) hath God to bring his people out by, yet all are but one in the end. This is, that he may be looked to from all the ends of the earth, to be a guide and lawgiver; and that none should judge before him. Deep is the mystery of godliness![17]

Thus in being inclusive, our theology must be concerned with our way of life, it must be moral, and it must be aware of, and try to avoid judging others.

In doing theology we are not setting up doctrines to be believed, but reflecting on our lives and experiences to see what can be shared. Our theology should be an enabler, enabling us to avoid hurtful dispute and enter into creative dialogue, to rejoice at the many ways in which God is known, and to enter continually into a loving fellowship with each other. Above all it should enable us to respond more fully to God, as the divine work and purpose is more clearly understood.

As we proceed on this venture you will see that four major questions are raised which need further discussion and development within the Society. These are the need to consider the question of truth, what is its nature, how may it be expressed, and what is its relationship to morality? The need to seek a new definition of humanity; the need to seek new ways of explaining the work and person of Jesus; and the need to reconsider what we may say about God. These are the areas I commend to your attention.

In our thinking we have to adopt an attitude that is based on both security and detachment. We are secure in our relationship to that eternal truth in whom we trust and live. But we must detach ourselves from any particular interpretation of, or statement about, that truth until we have considered whether or not we can accept it.

Ian Barbour writes:

> I would submit that religious commitment can indeed be combined with critical reflection. Commitment alone without enquiry tends to become fanaticism or narrow dogmatism; reflection alone without commitment tends to become trivial speculation unrelated to real life. Perhaps personal involvement must alternate with reflection on that involvement, since worship and critical enquiry at their most significant levels do not occur simultaneously. It is by no means easy to hold beliefs for which you would be willing to die, and yet to remain open to new insights; but it is precisely such a combination of commitment and enquiry that constitutes religious maturity.[18]

It is my faith that the Society of Friends is a religiously mature body, able to be both committed and searching for truth. So let us begin our enquiry.

The next step forward may be made by borrowing from science the concept of a model.

IV

OF TRUTH

I want to consider how we perceive the world. Some years ago we moved house, within the same village, a distance of no more than half a mile. A few days later I was walking through a part of the village which I knew well when I realised that it looked different. But I could see no changes in the houses or the landscape. Eventually I realised that the change was in my own mind, in my mental map. Always before, when I had walked that way, I had been oriented to my home, ahead on the left. Now I had a new home, behind on the right, and it had changed my whole perception of where I was.

Although the world exists outside ourselves, our knowledge of it does not exist separate from ourselves. For we make patterns in our minds and impose order on what we see. We decide what evidence is important and what can be ignored.

We sum up our experiences and attitudes in a set of mental constructs or models which help us to interpret and live in the world.

Sometimes we hold two models more or less simultaneously. There is a simple example of this in the relationship of the earth and the sun. In one model, the sun goes round the earth, helping us to distinguish direction, east and west and time of day. This model is reflected in language such as 'rising and setting' used of the sun.

In the other model we see the earth circling around the sun and part of the vast universe. There is a sense in which this model is more 'true', meaning here perhaps more scientific, but it is only necessary if we are astronomers or space-travellers. It will not help us find our way home if we are lost.

17

The former model is more 'true' to that experience in which we feel ourselves to be the centre of the universe and see everything as relative to ourselves. We can hold both these models in our minds as long as we do not get confused about which one to use at which time.

Now a model must be seen to be a model; it is not to be taken as a literal or an adequate picture of reality; it represents aspects of the truth; it cannot tell the whole truth; and it is not itself the truth. It is a tool for interpreting and restructuring experience. And it is also a way of working out what to expect. Thus with every model we come to a moment of crisis when what happens is not in accordance with what the model led us to believe was or would be the case.

At these times we must either alter our model or, occasionally, abandon it altogether in favour of a new one. Sometimes we can do this easily but at other times it can cause great anguish. This is nowhere more true than in religious matters where the joys of insight must be paid for by the tension that comes from our mind being out of step with our emotions.

For religious models are very significant to us. They not only state how we perceive the world but they involve our own place in it. The evidence on which they are based comes from our deepest experiences, and the models call for our deepest commitment not only in thought but in emotion and action. In a very real sense, we bet our lives on them.

Thus to criticise or change our models can be a very painful process. But we must remember that the models are only ways of representing truth, not truth itself. If we elevate our models beyond the reach of criticism we are in danger of making them into 'graven images', all the more dangerous because they are not visible.

In what sense, then, can we say that a model is true? At first, we might want to try the answer that a model is true if it is the 'best fit' with our experience. But this is too simple. For the way in which we view our experience, our selection of what is important and what is trivial, is already affected by the model we hold, which has been passed to us by our parents, our education, and our society. This is why, in the experience of the Jews at least, the most profound religious thinking has emerged from traumatic experiences of suffering, when the old models are shown to be inadequate and must be developed or replaced.

The problem is further complicated by the fact that when we look at other religions we see that there are many 'best fits' which are intellectually satisfying even if they do not suit our own temperaments or traditions. Can we have many 'true' models?

A Zoroastrian idea may help us here. The writer of Shikand Gumani Vazar points out that there are two types of opposites.[19] There are those whose opposition is one of function, such as male and female, which though they may be different cannot live without each other. And those opposites such as light and darkness which cannot exist simultaneously and are mutually destructive. So perhaps we can look at models and see if they can exist together or if they destroy each other.

Is there value in recognising that there are a number of models of the truth? Our answer must be yes. When we say this, we are saying, first, that no one form of words, no one concept, no one belief or set of beliefs can possibly contain or describe the whole of God's truth. And this is true to Quaker experience.

Secondly, we become open to growth and development as we recognise that our intellectual views are provisional and are not unchallenged. We realise that there are choices. Thus we are able to take part in theology as a process.

Thirdly, our freedom is preserved by other people's freedom. Whenever one belief gains a monopoly position in a state it seems to seek to uphold itself by persecution. When we look at the sad history of mankind, and unfortunately at the sad present, we see so many examples of attempts to crush minorities. The freedom to be different is very precious and very fragile.

Fourthly, choice preserves our free will and integrity towards God. It is consistent with a concept of God as wishing us to enter freely into relationship. As Barbour says, 'God safeguards our freedom by leaving room for more than one interpretation.'[20]

If we are to maintain our Quaker principles we must acknowledge that there are many models of the truth and that it is right that this is so. However, we must still consider the problem of how we judge models. Have we any ways of showing that some models are better, or more true, than others?

There are two criteria which may act as guides; these are rationality and morality. If we ask of a model that it be rational we make a number of demands upon it. It should be logical and internally coherent (thus it may not say both that there is only one God and that there are two Gods). It should be consistent with contemporary knowledge and thought or with the best of human thought (thus it may not say that creation occurred in 4004 BC, which is inconsistent with science, or that Jesus never lived, which is inconsistent with history). It should take into account the major problems of human life (thus it may not state that the world is good without attempting to explain suffering). Even so, rationality must be a guide rather than a rule, so that we may be open to the exploration of new possibilities.

The second criterion, that of morality, is expressed in the words of Jesus, 'By their fruits ye shall know them.' (*Matthew*, 7:16.) In looking at any model or system of belief we can judge it by its effects. What are its effects on the believer? Does it encourage maturity, does it strengthen, does it lead to freedom to hear and follow the leadings of God (under whatever name)? Or does it batten on people's weaknesses and encourage them to

20

WHAT CANST THOU SAY?

become dependent and give up their moral and intellectual autonomy?

Even more important, what does this model encourage people to do to others? How can we regard as true a belief, however reasonable it may sound, which encourages people to kill, torture, enslave or exploit their fellow human beings?

'For he that loveth not his brother whom he hath seen, cannot love God whom he hath not seen.' (*1 John*, 4:20.) This insistence on moral behaviour as a sign of right religion is a mark of early Quakerism. We have already seen Fox's insistence that the spirit leads to righteousness and unity. In an early document (1651), a letter to a magistrate, Elizabeth Hooton wrote, 'O friend, if the love of God was in you, you would love the truth and hear the truth spoken and not prison unjustly. . . . If the love of God had broken your heart, you would show mercy; but you do show forth what ruleth you.'[21]

William Penn wrote, 'But I think, we may without offence say, that since true religion gives men greater mildness and goodness than they had before, that religion that teaches them less, must needs be false.'[22]

However, whilst this may seem a simple rule and one well authorised, we must again be careful in its application. Firstly, we must not underestimate the human ability to distort belief systems and to use them to legitimise power and tyranny. Is what human beings do in the name of beliefs a real reflection of their truth?

If we apply this rule strictly, we may find that practically every belief is ruled out. All have been guilty in their time. And the record of Christianity is particularly shameful. It has approved and carried out wars and persecutions, the Inquisition, the burnings of heretics and witches and Jews.

But let not Quakers be too smug. We may, in England, have done nothing worse than disown a few people for 'marrying out'

21

or bankruptcy. We have seldom had the power to do more. How do we know that we would be immune from temptation? A pamphlet written against us in 1657 said, 'The Quaker's way is too cruel and uncharitable to be the way of God. They damn the most humble, holy, faithful servants of God; to whom God has promised salvation. All the ministers and Churches of Christ that adhere to the ministry, they pronounce them, children of the devil.'[23] And if you read certain of Fox's Epistles (notoriously 171, 172) you will see that 'uncharitable' is the right word.

Secondly, we must remember that morality is itself a changeable concept and that there are times when moral values clash. We do not condemn Christianity because Christians once held slaves, but we would if it now encouraged slavery. Jesus himself clashed with the accepted moral standards of his time.

We see therefore that morality is not an easy guide and raises the question of whether a belief can be judged by the behaviour of its adherents. Nevertheless, we must consider whether any belief can exist apart from its adherents. The way in which people model the world and the way in which they behave are intimately connected. Religions are not matters of belief which stand above and apart from and separate from their believers; they are also ways of life.

Perhaps we might agree that these two criteria, rationality and morality, are ideals for which to strive. They are standards by which we might rigorously judge our own faith and practice, but must be charitably applied to the beliefs or models of others. For it does seem that the worst excesses of religious zeal spring from the conviction that one is uniquely right and that others are therefore wrong. We might express it paradoxically as, 'to be right is wrong'.

So we shall find that even when we have rejected those models which are clearly non-rational or non-moral there are still many competing models of the truth; models which may contradict each other but which are each individually valid, each being a best human attempt to explain the mysteries of religion. We may prefer one model, because of our temperament, or upbringing, or culture, but we cannot deny the validity of the other models to those who hold them.

We thus see that there may be simultaneous models[24] in religion, explaining the same or similar phenomena differently, and issuing in similar, though culture-bound, ways of life. No one model in itself can contain the whole truth: each is only an interpretation, a guide to the spirit beyond itself and beyond all.

So that in seeking to know and express that spirit we may find that truth lies in paradox, in the tension between truths, in the presence of certainty simultaneously with ambiguity, in the tightrope between belief and experience, in the kaleidoscope of rationality, of feeling, of faith and action which yet revolves round its one unknowable centre.

As Damaris Parker-Rhodes said in the title of her Swarthmore Lecture, truth is a path and not a possession. We find that we are travelling on a living way, but the way itself is our goal and the end of our journey.

'The point,' says David Jenkins, 'is to live with paradox not to resolve it,'[25] to live in wrestling with it and in tension with it. We join the heritage of Israel, 'he who wrestles with God'; the struggle to explore the meaning of God and God's relationship with the world.

Let us explore some examples of what it means to live with paradox, that is, with two contradictory models of the truth.

As Quakers we believe that the whole of life is sacramental, that every place, person and action is potentially holy, that rituals are not necessary to bring us into the presence of God. But how do we know what this means? I learnt what it means to say that a place is holy in the Church of the Holy Sepulchre in Jerusalem, when I saw Christian women from all over the world

23

kneeling with tears in their eyes to kiss a slab of stone where they believed the body of Jesus had lain. Such reverence, such devotion, such humility, such grief, such depth of love as they showed must challenge us.

We are right, I am sure, to say that the whole world is holy, but we need others to tell us what this means. We cannot understand our own belief without reference to their actions or without using their words. At the same time, however, the church needs us to uphold the sacramental nature of the world. For in focusing on symbols and moments of holiness, there is a danger of separation of sacred and secular. Thus we need each other for the whole to be more truly expressed. Both aspects are true, but neither is sufficient by itself. Our task here is to uphold a truth, even whilst knowing it to be partial, for the sake of the greater whole.

Another paradox is often seen in the history of religion. How often is there a conflict between the truth which is known and cherished, and the new insights brought about by new situations or new teachers. We see it as the conflict between priest and prophet, between established churches and religious reformers. Perhaps most of all we see it in the conflicts between Jesus and the religious men of his time. But do not judge the Pharisees and Sadducees too harshly; they too are our brothers; indeed, if the truth be known, they may be more our kind than Jesus was. They were men with a knowledge of God to preserve, with a way of life to prosper, with a nation to tend. They were courageous in protecting their beliefs against an occupying power, they were faithful in carrying out their religious duties, they tried to discourage political hotheads who would bring down destruction on the nation and the faith; they, too, were part of God's purposes. In following the truth as they saw it they exposed their people in time to a campaign of vilification and persecution of which all Christians should feel ashamed. We can

24

see God's suffering servants as truly in Israel as in Christ.[26]

We must resist the temptation to come down on one side or the other. We are not for the preservers of tradition, we are not for the iconoclasts. We have found in our business meetings where we take no votes but try to reach the right solution with which all can agree, that by living in the tension between views it is possible to reach new solutions that we had not considered before. By living with paradox we are not 'sitting on the fence' but seeking a creative way forward which does not judge people and their differences but uses and goes beyond them. We live with a constant recreation of truth.

*   *   *

We shall use these concepts which we have explained to explore three areas of theology.

Firstly, we shall look at Christianity and the models used to explain the person of Jesus and discuss which of these models meet the criteria suggested, and what new models might be developed.

Secondly, we shall use the concept of simultaneous models to approach the problem of Quaker relationships with Christianity and other religions.

Thirdly we shall use the concept of simultaneous models to explore ways of talking about God.

We shall, I hope, see that this is a most fruitful approach to theology, which is consistent with Quaker principles, appropriate to the methods of theology, able to cast light on (if not to solve) problems from the past and to indicate new directions for the future.

Va

OF HOPE

We come then to Christianity. But what is Christianity? It is systems of belief, ways of life, groups organised into churches, history, culture; it is all and none of these. Christianity is not a monolith; it is not a single unchanging system; it never has been. Even in the earliest days it was divided into groups, riven by quarrels, and producing many different explanations and theologies.

The saying 'Thou art Peter and on this rock will I build my church' may or may not be from Jesus, but whoever said it shows an insight into the nature of the church. The Jewish Temple was built on rock, bedrock, very solid, stable, firm, unmoving, unchanging, dead. But the Christian church is built on the living rock of humanity, fallible, unreliable, turncoat, quarrelsome, misunderstanding, but capable of rising to great heights of insight, love and self-sacrifice. So there are many facets of Christianity, many Christianities. And the question I mentioned earlier 'Are Quakers Christian?' becomes altered. It is not whether we are Christians but what sort of Christians we are. Or, if I may put it in a very chauvinist way, what sort of Christianity is compatible with Quaker experience of and insight into the truth?

The major questions in Christianity revolve around the person and work of Jesus. Who was he and what did he do? They are questions which every age has tried to answer and which we too must answer for ourselves. In setting out to do this we do not denigrate the answers reached in the past. All human experience of truth must be respected. But we do not thereby simply accept what we are told. The age of an idea is no

27

guarantee that it is right. If we measured truth by age we should have to accept slavery and war, those millennia-old institutions, as being right, but we do not. George Fox posed the question, 'What canst thou say?' It is the task of each person to answer it. Nor, in raising again the questions about Jesus, do we in any way denigrate him. We do not dispute that he was a man who truly followed the leadings of the spirit, who was a profound religious teacher and who has inspired many millions of people. There is no question but that he was an outstanding man and that God acted through him. The very fact that he is still discussed and referred to shows this. But was he more than this and did he do more than this? What was his significance?

The first answers to this question were shaped in a world very different from our own; a world that saw nothing wrong with slavery, though ethical people believed they should treat their slaves well; a world which thought in mythological terms, which saw nothing odd in declaring a man to be a god; a world which had no intellectual problem over miracles; a world whose thought-forms and language were different from ours, and whose perceptions of the nature of man and the world were not ours.

The early church faced with the experiences which they named the resurrection and Pentecost, sought explanations which made sense in terms of the models of the world which they held. Now we are in a situation where our world-models have changed. For example, we no longer seriously think of God as residing in a heaven above the sky. But our language inherited from the past is out of phase with our understanding and experience. Our mild-mannered constitutional monarchs give a different meaning to 'Christ the King' from the awe and majesty and terror which that phrase first suggested.

So we must look at the models which the early church held and used to explain Jesus. When we have understood what they were trying to say, we can see how far it accords with our own experience and perceptions; that is, how far we can accept it and how far we must interpret it anew.

We shall look at three early models, the Christ, the Saviour, and the Trinity, all of which are under discussion in contemporary theology.

One of the outstanding features of the New Testament documents, one that appears alien to much twentieth-century thought, is the eschatological expectation, the hope that God will soon act in defeating evil. Language such as 'the Kingdom of God' and 'Messiah/Christ' is closely connected with this expectation. Let us see how and why it arose.

The original Jewish experience of God was as one who was active in history as a saviour. This was the significance of the Exodus, still commemorated in the Passover. To this was added, with the idea of the Covenant, the concept of God as just and righteous. Psalmsingers and prophets took this further. They used metaphors from their own experience to portray God as a husband, a king, a parent, a shepherd, who was tender and merciful.[27]

In contact with other nations, the Jews expanded this concept until God was also seen as creator of the whole world, controller of all nations, and responsible for good and evil.[28]

But monotheism brings one supreme problem—with such a God as this, how can life in the world be so unsatisfactory—in particular, how can there be so much pain, death, frustration and suffering?

In the Old Testament we find many attempts to answer this problem. One of the first solutions was that suffering was a punishment for sin. The writer of the story of the garden of Eden blamed the sin on the ancestors (*Genesis*, 2 and 3); historical writers blamed it on the community which worshipped false gods, and on the king as representative of the people who

29

allowed them to go astray and break the covenant (e.g. *II Kings*, 21:11-15).

Now whilst these views preserved one important truth, that the community suffers together, by the sixth century BC they were being criticised. It was seen that for an individual to be punished for the sins of others was not only unjust but destroyed the basis of personal morality. The prophets Jeremiah and Ezekiel both declared that the individual was responsible and should suffer for his own sins (*Jeremiah*, 31:29-30; *Ezekiel*, 18).

But this too did not fully meet the case. How could one explain the suffering of a righteous individual? The book of Job in particular tries to answer this question, suggesting, amongst other solutions, that suffering may be a test of piety, and that it is impossible to understand the ways of God.

The prophet whom we call Second Isaiah suggests, poetically rather than in any worked-out philosophical view, that suffering, while remaining inexplicable, may be redemptive for others if willingly borne (*Isaiah*, 52:13-53:12).

In the last two centuries before Jesus the problem became more acute when Jews were persecuted by foreign rulers such as Antiochus Epiphanes for being faithful to the laws and practices of Judaism. How could one justify the deaths of these righteous?

An answer was shaping itself. It was made of many strands, not the least of which was the old conviction that God was ruler over history who would one day act on the 'Day of the Lord'.

Another strand came from the contact with the Persians who followed Zoroaster. Although normative Judaism always rejected Zoroastrian dualism and saw God as responsible for both good and evil, many Jews were attracted by the concept of a final battle between good and evil when God would ultimately triumph and set up a new type of society, the kingdom of God on earth. They also took from Zoroastrianism the idea of resurrection of the dead and final judgement. In this way they 'solved' the problem of suffering by postponing God's righteous actions and judgement to the future.

From Greek and Persian thought they also took the idea that God would work through intermediaries, thus developing not only an angelology but a supernatural side to the old idea of God's anointed ruler, the Messiah.

Very little of this is found in the Old Testament, but there is a good deal in the inter-testamental literature and in the Dead Sea Scrolls, in the type of literature that is described as 'apocalyptic'.

By the time of Jesus, Jewish thought is permeated by an eschatological expectation of the end, and this is used to interpret the work of Jesus. Thus his healings are seen as part of the battle between good and evil; the disciples' experience of him after his death is interpreted as the first fruits of the final resurrection—it is not that he has come back to life but that he has gone through and beyond death into the life of the world to come; and one of the first titles that he is given is Messiah/Christ (the anointed one), that is, God's intermediary and ruler when the end time comes.

Now do we, or should we, accept this model? The value of eschatological expectation is its radical discontent. It sets up against the present order of life, both political and religious, a vision of transformation, of new values, of a new community. It is a theology of hope. It never allows us to be content with the life we have but always points to a standard which criticises our actions and values. Nevertheless, the future is not to be achieved by human action but by divine grace. This critical spirit, and hope for the future, is valuable. But the eschatological model can have other consequences which are not so desirable.

It can lead to a neglect of present social conditions and a concentration on individual piety; a feeling that if only God can right wrongs the individual need not bother, that justice cannot

31

be achieved in this world so may be postponed, that our task is not to relieve oppression but to be worthy of our own place in the kingdom.

There is enough biblical evidence to suggest that Jesus was scathing of such attitudes. For example, in the parable of the sheep and the goats the criteria by which people are judged are entirely concerned with practical, moral behaviour; religiosity and belief play no part in their salvation (*Matthew*, 25).

Secondly, eschatology can be escapist. Fohrer says it 'is the desire to be delivered from history and the necessities of everyday life.'[29] But history, as the Jews discovered, is where we meet and know God. The desire to escape from the struggle, to postpone God's action to the future, is essentially atheistic. It seeks to avoid the knowledge of God and the relationship with God which is available to us now. The present is the only time we have—this is where we meet God. And the knowledge of God which we gain in this meeting is itself sufficient to provide both the divine discontent and the hope for the future which eschatology provides; and the spur to action which it does not. The sense of God as transcendent provides a critique of all human life against ultimate reality; whilst the sense of God as immanent shows that it is proper to be involved in loving, creative change.

Thirdly, eschatology does not adequately answer the problem of the unsatisfactoriness of life and the presence of suffering which was the cause of its development. It postpones God's righteousness and justice to a far distant future. But if God is to be exonerated it must be in the world as it is, in the lives of individuals and communities as they are.

The eschatological model cannot be satisfactory because it accepts a concept of God which is less than the best we know. All its most valuable points, about hope, can be expressed in other ways by developing a more adequate model of God.

The eschatological expectation was already being found un-

32

satisfactory in New Testament times. We find in the gospels a tension between the idea of the kingdom of God as a future state and the idea of it as a present state. So that it is equally biblical to suggest that we are living in the kingdom of God[30]—as long as we are careful not to identify it with the institutional church!

One of the most profound understandings of the kingdom of God is in Mark's gospel. The author of Mark, writing probably for a church that had met persecution and was faced by the problem of suffering and meaningless death in its most acute form, reinterpreted the idea of God's kingdom to show it was being achieved not by power and triumph but by the death of Jesus on the cross.

We are warned of this interpretation by the use made of the saying, 'There be some here of them that stand by, which shall in no wise taste of death, till they see the kingdom of God come with power' (*Mark*, 9:1). This is set in the context of the central incident of Peter's confession when the need to suffer is explained. So that we have the kingdom linked with suffering and are warned that it is soon to happen.

We may see too a significance in the placing in chapter 14, verses 3 to 9, of the anointing of Jesus. It is the only anointing in Mark, and it is an anointing for burial. Mark thus gives a whole new meaning to the title Messiah/Christ.

Mark drops hints that the day of the crucifixion is the day of the Lord expected by the prophets, by incorporating into his account references to the book of Amos. The young man (*Mark*, 14:51-2) who flees from Gethsemane can be seen in terms of (*Amos*, 2:16)—'he that is courageous among the mighty shall flee away naked in that day.'[31] And the darkness from the sixth to the ninth hour (*Mark*, 15:33) reflects (*Amos*, 5:18 and 20)— 'shall not the day of the Lord be darkness, and not light? even very dark and no brightness in it?'

Another hint comes in the account of the last supper (*Mark*,

14:25) when Jesus is reported as saying 'I will no more drink of the fruit of the vine until that day when I drink it new in the kingdom of God.' In chapter 15, verse 36, Jesus' last act before he dies is shown as the drinking of vinegar, which was made from new, sour wine. Mark is telling us that this is the kingdom of God, this last moment of utter dereliction, despair and hopelessness, when Jesus is losing not only his life but his faith and confidence in God.

It is the cry, 'My god, my God, why hast thou forsaken me?' which clinches the matter. Mark expresses Jesus' final loneliness in the words of the twenty-second psalm. And when we compare the early part of that lament with his account of the crucifixion we see how he has used the words of the psalm in recording Jesus' plight. 'All they that see me laugh me to scorn: they shoot out the lip, they shake the head, saying, Commit thyself unto the Lord; let him deliver him.' (*Psalm*, 22:7-8.) 'They pierced my hands and my feet.' (*Psalm*, 22:16.) 'They part my garments among them.' (*Psalm*, 22:18.)

Yet the psalm, which underlies the crucifixion story, changes to a psalm of trust and praise. 'All the ends of the earth shall remember and turn unto the Lord and all the kindreds of the nations shall worship before thee. For the kingdom is the Lord's and he is the ruler over the nations.' (*Psalm*, 22:27-8.)

So that in reminding us of the psalm, Mark is referring to the end as well as the beginning. Thus the crucial verse in his account (*Mark*, 15:39) comes at the death of Jesus. 'When the centurion . . . saw that he so gave up the ghost he said, "Truly this man was the Son of God".'

The centurion, a gentile, stands for all the nations of the world turning to worship God. He is the first fruits of the kingdom and his confession comes about not because of a demonstration of glory but because of weakness and obedience. Mark is saying that what made Jesus the Son of God was his willingness to obey God, to follow the leadings of the spirit, even though they led not only to physical, but apparently to spiritual, death.

If we relate this to the problem of suffering with which we began our consideration of eschatology, Mark's theology suggests that no experience of pain or degradation or despair can alienate God's love from us; and that it is precisely here, in the willing bearing of suffering, and the setting aside of self that God's rule is made manifest and effective. The kingdom is present in every loving heart and selfless act.

Mark further shows that no human evil or mistake can prevent the purposes of God. God can make use of every situation, however ugly or horrible, to reach out to people and call them into the kingdom.

From the human point of view it was the death of Jesus on the cross and the subsequent interpretation of it which brought about this understanding of the nature and activity of God. However, we cannot say that this event made any change in the nature of God for, if God is and was 'the same for ever', then the 'kingdom' has always been available and God has always been concerned in suffering from the beginning of time. God's purpose does not change, though our understanding of it does.

Thus in exploring the eschatological model we have I think seen that it does not satisfactorily explain the nature of God or the work of Jesus; our explanation has led us, however, to a deeper understanding of God. I would suggest then that the model which saw Jesus as the Christ, the ruler in a future kingdom, must be rejected. Instead we see that God is our hope. Further, this hope is not only for the future but for the present, for God has already acted, is present with us in all the circumstances of our lives, calling us to be open to the spirit of love.

Vb

OF SALVATION

One of the most important of the models used to describe the work of Jesus is the concept 'Saviour'. Though the use of the term developed late in the New Testament Paul expressed the concept through four remarkable metaphors which were relevant to his world though somewhat strange to ours.

He described Jesus as a redeemer, that is, one who buys others out of slavery (e.g. *1 Corinthians*, 6:20). He used a legal model, describing him as one who takes the punishment due to another (e.g. *Romans*, 4:25). He used the cultic picture of a sacrifice offered to propitiate a deity (e.g. *Romans*, 3:25). He went back also to the Genesis myth of Adam and Eve (which we have seen was an attempt to explain suffering) and reinterpreted it seeing the work of Jesus as being that of a second Adam who brought life where the first had brought death (e.g. *1 Corinthians*, 15:22).

But what began as pictures, springing from the glorious sense of release and freedom felt by the early church, in time came to be taken as literal explanations of what had happened on a supernatural plane. With the adoption of the canon and the view that the scriptures were divinely revealed, rigid interpretations were developed.

Thus Augustine of Hippo wrote that since 'from Adam derives the alienation from God which affects the whole human race, all men are, as it were, one lump of sin, incurring the punishment of the supreme justice of God.'[32]

Augustine affirmed that men were predestined either to eternal mercy or eternal punishment, and though this was not accepted throughout the church, it surfaced again in the sixteenth century in the teachings of John Calvin.

So that we find that in considering what is meant by calling Jesus a saviour, we are also involved in considering both human nature and the human predicament, and the character of God.

The story of Adam and Eve can in no sense be regarded as literally true. But in using it, the church was trying to wrestle with and explain the problem of human nature and human community. We know that human beings, either intentionally or unintentionally, can be cruel or oppressive, can have all the faults of pride, selfishness and greed which have traditionally been called sin. And we must never underestimate this aspect of our lives. But can we go so far as to say that human nature is so sinful that all deserve punishment?

In fact, the testimony of the Society from the beginning has rejected the Calvinistic view and has assumed the possibility of salvation for all. 'Fox could not accept any description of man's nature that takes away his responsibility for sin by making him incapable of doing good, nor accept any view of God's relation to man in which God's demand that people shall be righteous can be satisfied by righteousness imputed to them.'[33]

In this century, Edward Grubb repeated this point. 'It is not true. The doctrine of total human depravity had its sole foundation in a literal interpretation of certain texts of scripture; it is contradicted by all our experience of life and by the plain teaching of the Master Himself. ... We cannot possibly admit that man, as man, is hopelessly corrupt and dark.'[34]

What then is our experience? Is it not of the possibilities of goodness? As we have learnt more of how people interact with each other and of how they respond to the expectations of others, we now know that people tend to become what we expect them to be.[35] Thus, if we regard people as fundamentally sinful, that is what they are likely to become. If we regard them as capable of love and goodness and trust, these are the capacities that they develop. We know as a Society that our belief in that

38

of God in everyone has enabled us to find it and has led to spiritual growth—not only in the individual but in our meetings. So that what we believe about human nature is part of the complex process of the 'becoming' of human nature. How can we then believe in anything other than basic goodness?

What we believe about human nature also affects the way in which we treat each other and thus our beliefs have moral consequences for ourselves as well as others. The worst effects of belief in sin and damnation have come from the excuse it provides for punishment and repression. The belief that others are different and that they are hated by God has been the rationalisation for the persecution of heretics and witches and Jews. The converse, that people must believe in order to be saved, has supported the Inquisition and that type of paternalistic evangelism that led directly to colonialism and exploitation. One of the worst results of the use of the myth of Adam and Eve is the way that it has been used to defend the subordination of women. With teachings such as Paul's letter to Timothy (2:11-14) where women are not allowed to teach because Eve was deceived, and the writings of Tertullian who blamed women for the death of Christ,[36] the church denied women social, economic and political rights and denigrated both their sexuality and their spirituality. Even now, the largest part of the church denies, in action if not in words, the spiritual and moral capacities of women.

Taken to the extreme, any belief that human beings are incapable of goodness destroys the motivation for moral actions and makes a mockery of our experience that there are many people who are good, loving, caring and responsible.

We need to think again about human nature, both in its sinfulness and its goodness, seeking for a description which will be both true to experience and a basis for ethical interaction.

The parable of the two sons may help here—it is usually

known as 'the Prodigal Son', but it is in fact about two brothers, the elder of whom, who is often neglected, stayed close to the father and worked for him. And despite his annoyance at the reception given to the returning prodigal, he was reassured by the father, 'Child, you are always with me and all that is mine is yours.' Though the brothers were different in their motivations and their actions we should not stress the difference. They were brothers and there was room for both in the father's house. Any way of looking at human nature must seek the unity between us. In our goodness and our sins we are all the children of God.

It seems then that the traditional expression of the concept of Jesus as saviour involves an unacceptable view of human nature. In looking at the pictures of the punished, the redeemer, and the sacrifice, we may see that these also involve an unacceptable view of God. For from what can we say that Jesus saves us? It cannot be from death, for we still die; nor from sin, for we still sin; nor from suffering for not only do we still suffer but we have seen that we cannot regard suffering as a punishment for sin.

If we see Jesus as redeeming or buying us out of the power of sin, we are suggesting that there is a power as strong as God. If we see him as a sacrifice, we are suggesting that God is a wrathful, vengeful deity who has to be bought off with the blood of the innocent. How can we accept such notions? They had already been rejected more than seven centuries before Jesus. 'For I desire mercy and not sacrifice; and the knowledge of God more than burnt offerings.' (*Hosea*, 6:6).[37]

And they contradict the teaching of Jesus in his approval of the scribe's saying (*Mark*, 12:32-34): 'There is one God, and there is none other than he; and to love him with all the heart and with all the understanding and with all the soul, and with all the strength, and to love one's neighbour as oneself, is more than whole burnt offerings and sacrifices.'

These pictures may have had striking force for the early

church, but for us their literal interpretation is inadequate and they have lost the concrete meaning in our lives which would give them metaphorical value. We cannot then use them.

Can we, however, say that Jesus was Saviour because he demonstrated the love of God and in so doing caused people to turn to God and seek reconciliation? We can say this, but it is by now a very different statement. It implies that the death of Jesus brought about no fundamental change in God's saving will; that is, that it was always God's intention to save. So that the death of Jesus was not necessary for salvation.

It also implies, from the very fact that the knowledge of Jesus is not worldwide, that this is not the only means of reconciliation and thus is not necessary to reconciliation.

Jesus may be called 'Saviour' but only in the sense that he leads us towards the salvation which is offered by God. Any other interpretation runs into profound difficulties.[38]

With this conclusion, let us start again to look at salvation and the concomitant question of the nature of humankind. From what do we need to be saved and what is the salvation we desire?

We live in an ambiguous world, which can be interpreted as happening by design or by chance; which can be seen as full of beauty and goodness, or suffering and evil; in which we can find divine purpose or complete absurdity. We experience ourselves in this world in a conflict between responsibility and impotence; in a situation of creation and destruction, anxiety and hope. We are finite creatures with a knowledge of our finitude, but with immortal longings. We know ourselves subject to time, and with it, to change, growth, decay, frustration, pain and death. Perhaps above all we wish to be saved from being meaningless.

We know ourselves as individuals but only because we live in community. Love, trust, fellowship, selflessness are all mediated to us through our interdependence. Just as we could not live physically without each other, we cannot live spiritually in isolation. We are individually free but also communally bound. We cannot act without affecting others and others cannot act without affecting us. We know ourselves as we are reflected in the faces, actions and attitudes of each other.

We can only separate ourselves from the community after it has formed us and we cannot think of ourselves except by reference to the community and its ways of thought and speech.

Both the individual and the community are free to go wrong and to learn from their mistakes, but the community differs from the individual in that its wrongdoings are magnified in their effects, but its powers of self-renewal are greater (very seldom does a community 'die').

Let us suppose that this was how God intended it to be. From what then do we wish to be saved? We are back to the problem that faced the writer of the myth, that of pain, suffering, frustration and death, and of the evil that we can inflict on one another, often unintentionally. We are, in fact, querying our humanity and asking in what way it accords with God's purposes. Now I cannot solve the problem of suffering. It has occupied mankind for millennia.[39] But perhaps I can comment on what appear to be its purposes, in relation to the question of salvation.

One aspect of the problem is that we are subject to death, often unpredictable. There is little comfort to those who have lost the ones they love, especially if these are children who have had no opportunity of reaching maturity. But our subjection to time is a condition of growth. We cannot change without time, and without the knowledge of death we cannot reach what Heidegger called 'authentic being'.

Only because of time and death do we have the chance to reach spiritual maturity. Without the trauma of birth, how could we ever have known love and sharing, and sorrow and joy?

When we have gone through death what more shall we know?

The second aspect of the problem is the evil that we do to one another, the suffering that we inflict whether in wars or murder, or more indirectly by starvation and exploitation. How can a powerful and just God permit us to do such things? And how can a loving God prevent us? Does the analogy of the parent help here? When our child is ready to walk we do not stop it even though we know that it will tumble and hurt itself. And as our children grow older we accept that they must grow away from us and live for themselves if they are to be complete people. Even if we could prevent some of their mistakes we know that they can only learn by living through their own experience.

In the second century AD Irenaeus took the view that 'Man has first to come into being, then to progress, and by progressing to come to manhood, and having reached manhood to increase, and thus increasing to persevere, and by persevering be glorified, and thus see his Lord.' He suggested that God created us knowing our weaknesses but that this was the only way in which we might reach perfection.

In this century this point of view has re-emerged. Leonard Hodgson wrote:

> If we can believe that the aim of creation is the production of persons whose goodness is the perfection of freedom, it makes sense to regard their permission to be wicked in the course of their making as incidental to the achievement of that purpose.
>
> And if at times we are appalled by the depths to which, in the history of this world, wickedness has been allowed to descend, and the extent to which it has been allowed to prevail, I can see no light in the darkness except by taking these depths and this extent as the measure of the value set by God upon the created freedom being genuinely free.[40]

43

Does God then leave us free to learn and grow? If so, at what a cost! The cost is paid by the innocent, the hurt, the damaged in body, mind and spirit. Is it also paid by God? What does it cost God to leave us free? Can we only find worthy of worship a God who grieves with our grief, suffers with our pain, who is involved with us in the terrors and complexities of our lives?

What then is salvation? How can it be an escape from death and suffering if these are so costly that only absolute necessity could excuse them? We must not look on God as one who will rescue us from our troubles and perplexities. The very message of the cross is that God will not send an army of angels to remove our difficulties, but will be with us living through them.

So we should see salvation not as a saving *from* but as a saving *to*.

To what? How can we express the inexpressible? It is reconciliation with God; it is closeness to God's will and purposes; it is wholeness; it is reaching what we were intended to be.

And more than this. For just as the statue is formed by the removal of stone, so we are hewn out of our possibilities by our choices. In those moments when we know God's judgement we are enabled not so much to remove our imperfections as to turn to the shape of good. And this judgement, I suggest, is continuous rather than final. For when we are freed from the notion that judgement involves suffering as a punishment we may see that, paradoxically, God's judgement is not to be opposed to God's love and mercy. Beyond both these concepts there is a state where love is judgement and judgement is love.

And more than this. For we are enabled through the grace of God. It is God who shows us ourselves and gives us power to change and is constantly available to help in healing and renewal. In a sense, God continually creates us.

As Lampe says, 'Salvation is that part or aspect of the divine creative activity by which man comes to be informed by God's presence, made in his image and likeness, and led to respond with trust and willing obedience to the love and graciousness of his Creator.'[41]

And yet more than this. For as the individual cannot live without the community, we cannot be finally saved without the community. Salvation is for all, and until every last one is reconciled to God, is healed and is whole, then our own salvation is not complete.

In the past we have talked of the kingdom of God as the destination of the community and salvation as the destiny of the individual. But these are not different from each other. The kingdom of God is salvation and salvation is the kingdom of God.

> Reconciliation aims at the human race as a whole. It is as wide as creation and potentially all men are embraced within its outreach.
>
> This may not mean that all men must explicitly accept the particular symbols of the Christian revelation. We have already made clear our conviction that other faiths too have a revelation that comes from one God, and that can be therefore only a revelation that likewise leads to reconciliation.[42]

Thus we cannot believe in hell. As Hick explains, 'The doctrine of hell has as its implied premise either that God does not desire to save all His (*sic*) human creatures, in which case He is only limitedly good, or that His purpose has finally failed in the case of some—and indeed, according to the theological tradition, most—of them, in which case He is only limitedly sovereign. I therefore believe that the needs of Christian theodicy compel us to repudiate the idea of eternal punishment.'[43]

We must then go beyond Barclay, who said[44] that God had

given every man a measure of Light by which he invites, exhorts
and strives with man in order to save him. We go beyond to
suggest that God never ceases to desire and work for the salvation of each created person and that ultimately this loving
purpose will be successful.

But what a task faces the creator. What infinite care is needed
to 'heal our sorrows, bind our wounds'. And more, what infinite
pity for those who most need to be reconciled when they see
themselves as they are, when they cannot hide from themselves,
when they recognise the harm they have done, in wars and
murders, cruelty, slavery, oppression and hatred. What love will
be needed to make them whole.

They cannot be healed, and we cannot be healed without
mutual reconciliation and forgiveness. For we have made them
what they are. We have taught them fear and insecurity instead
of love and trust. We have permitted exploitation and torture, we
have washed our hands and declared our innocence.

Jesus was very clear that we cannot be reconciled with God
unless we are reconciled with our neighbour (*Matthew*, 5:23-24)
and that we cannot ask for forgiveness for ourselves until we
have forgiven (*Matthew*, 6:12, 14-15). The two great command-
ments that we love God and that we love our neighbour go
together.

We come here into another paradox. For whilst salvation and
the kingdom rest on the loving grace of God who does not need
us, yet we are called to be partakers in the work of bringing
about the kingdom. As we act in obedience to the Light within,
we may become mediators through whom God's love is known.

And so we are called to share the task of God, to share the
grief and the joy, the sorrow, the self-giving, and the reconciliation.

We are called upon to love the loveless and the unlovable, to
reach out to the racists and the torturers, to all who hurt and

damage, cripple and kill. They are God's unhappy children who need especial care. They have harmed themselves, but not irredeemably; and God, through us, and in many other ways, offers them healing love and divine pity and takes their hurts away.

We are called to that obedience which freely gives up self, possessions, life, beliefs, in following that vision, that greater love in which alone is life and peace. This does not mean that we lie down like doormats to be trampled on, or that we give up our freedom or our grasp of truth—it means that we join ourselves to the risk of creation, to the venture of authentic human being, that we 'stand in the Light', reveal that measure of truth that is known to us, are vehicles of God's disclosure which is both tender and terrible, gentle and bold, whose mercy is judgement; that we face the pain of the world, and match it with forgiveness.[45]

To do God's work we do not have to be good people. Moses was a runaway murderer, Jacob was a thief, Peter was impulsive and unreliable, Paul was bitter with hatred, but God could use them. Nor are we protected from being wrong. The family of Jesus thought he was 'beside himself' (*Mark*, 3:21); the early church was riven with quarrels; mistakes were made in doctrines which led to splits between churches. We know ourselves how easy it is, especially when we are feeling religious and inspired, to fall down on some act of kindness.

Our hope and confidence is not in ourselves but in God whose grace is sufficient to complete the work and whose self-giving love reaches out to us however unworthy we are.

When we face our own unworthiness, when we share with others the pain of self-knowledge, the pain of the world's brokenness, we find that at the heart of the darkness, at the profoundest depths of the human anguish, God is already present, already strengthening and comforting, already bearing our cross.

So that our weakness, our vulnerability, our sin when it is laid open to God and made subject to the light, is graciously accepted and used, becoming a means of service.

*   *   *

Thus it seems that we must reject the model of Jesus as Saviour for it is based on an inadequate concept of humanity and an inadequate concept of God, and it has had results which are morally objectionable. However, we have found in our exploration that it can be replaced by a model of God as saviour, who by grace is continually creating humanity into what it shall be.

Vc

OF RESPONSE

The third model describing Jesus that we must consider is that of the Trinity. This was the answer that the church developed to the problem of how Jesus is related to God—a problem which occupied the church from the beginning and still is fervently discussed.[46]

What the doctrine of the Trinity sets out to do is to make two simultaneous claims, the first that we know God in three ways, as creator of the world, as revealed in Jesus, and as the spirit which inspires the church; the second that there is nevertheless only one God.

In so far as it is a general statement which refers to experience it may be a valid expression of faith. It could indeed be viewed in terms of the simultaneous models discussed earlier.

But unfortunately the doctrine goes further than this. It tries to explain how it comes about that there is one God in three persons and in doing so traps us in the philosophy of the fourth century, in substance and accidents, in quasi-chemical formulae. The Athanasian Creed states: 'One God in Trinity and Trinity in Unity; neither confounding the Person nor dividing the Substance. For there is one person of the Father, another of the Son and another of the Holy Ghost. But the godhead of the Father, of the Son, and of the Holy Ghost, is all one.'

There are difficulties in this definition. One is that the words used by the Athanasians to describe Substance (homoousia) and Person (hypostasis) are not exact terms and when the creed was being formulated were taken to have different meanings by different groups. Indeed, I strongly suspect that the formulation

49

is successful only as long as no one asks too closely what it means.

Another difficulty is that although it relates Christ and God in godhead it leaves unsolved their relationship in manhood. There is still no satisfactory way of explaining how the human Jesus could also be the incarnate God.

Thus there are logical problems in holding this model. However, it does have some value. In trying to incorporate our different experiences of God it includes relationship in God and so sees in divinity some of the personal qualities we value in humanity. And it allows within one model for both the transcendence and the immanence of God and for our knowledge through revelation and experience. Any alternative model would need also to include these elements.

However the most pungent criticisms of the doctrine of the Trinity must be of its effects. It has caused many splits in the Christian church. During the decades when the debate about it took place, it was associated with the power struggle between bishops and bishoprics and involved the authority of the state. One historian wrote 'When (the Church) passed verdicts of condemnation, certain political consequences followed. Thus the Arians and the opposing bishops ... were not only excommunicated from the church, but also removed from their offices by the power of the state, and sent into exile.'[47] The Emperor Julian commented that 'Christians are more dangerous enemies to one another than wild beasts.'[48]

In the fifth century the oriental churches, the Syrians and Copts, were excommunicated by the Greek-speaking churches for holding that Jesus had one nature, the divine, and not two, divine and human.[49] In the eleventh century the Latin and Byzantine churches split partly over whether the spirit proceeded only from the Father or also from the Son. So that the urge to define God with precision has led not to unity but conflict in the church.

Can we also say that it causes a split between Christianity and other religions? Over the centuries the charge that the Jews killed God has led to horrific consequences. Muslims find it difficult to see how the Trinity can be reconciled with monotheism. If we are to say that all faiths worship essentially the same God, can we insist that this God includes Jesus? We surely cannot in this wider context say that any belief in Jesus is essential.

Hick says: 'It seems clear that we are being called today to attain a global religious vision which is aware of the unity of all mankind before God and which at the same time makes sense of the divinity of God's ways within the various streams of human life.'[50]

So it seems that the way in which this doctrine divides is because it puts the emphasis in the wrong place. It makes Christianity a matter of assenting to a belief, to a form of words, rather than a way of life which trusts in God and acts with love within the community.

Lastly, in effect though not admittedly in intention, it limits God. It gives the impression that God can be understood and described. But 'the nature of God is incommensurable with human ways of thought.'[51] We come always to the point where words fail, where definitions are inadequate, where *omnia exeunt in mysterium*.

We must consider then that the doctrine of the Trinity is a model that must now be rejected. As Gerald Hibbert said in the 1924 Swarthmore Lecture: 'After a building has reached a certain height we no longer need the scaffolding. The conception of the Trinity as worked out by the later Fathers of the Church seems to me an example of that mechanical way of looking at things . . .'[52]

We have then reached a point where our investigations

51

suggest that there is no need in Quakerism for a doctrine of redemption through Christ or a doctrine of the Trinity, because these doctrines inadequately represent God, the living, loving, saving Spirit we have experienced. We must instead begin to look for new ways of expressing truth.

Some Friends may find this conclusion slightly shocking, not least because if Christianity is defined by these doctrines, then we cannot be Christians. But we have never set much store by doctrines, nor can they be a full definition of Christianity. We may discover that we are reluctant to give up old ways of thought. This is partly through fear, partly what we may term nostalgia.

There is a lingering, superstitious fear of what God will do to us if we do not placate him with the right words, the right beliefs and the right actions. But this is the old idea of the angry, capricious monster that we must firmly reject. We must trust in the light that we have. John Macmurray wrote, 'All religions deal with fear. They promise security and protection to their followers. In effect they say, "There is nothing to be afraid of." But usually when they say this they mean that if you believe in God and perform your religious duties, God will protect you from the things you are afraid of. And this is an idealistic illusion. Jesus was a realist. He knew that it was the fear itself that had to be dealt with.'[53]

The love of God casts out fear. True religion consists not in right belief but in right relationship.

'Nostalgia' is even more powerful. For centuries people have believed in these doctrines and lived their lives, as they thought, by them. They have expressed their faith in music and art and buildings that are beautiful and can affect us deeply. When a glorious soprano voice rings out 'I know that my redeemer liveth', we are caught up in the powerful symbolism—even when we know that it is a misinterpretation of what the original writer meant. The symbols attached to redemption, to the crucified God, are very compelling and part of our culture. This can have value but it can also imprison us. Thus I feel that early Friends followed a true instinct in avoiding the arts especially in religion and worship. Beauty is not the same as truth. It may hint at truth, it may illuminate truth, but it may also ossify or obscure it.

We must hold to our symbols lightly, for as long as they are helpful, but let them go gracefully as we seek new interpretations. For the power lies not in the symbols themselves but in the Spirit which they try to represent. It is the Spirit we seek.

So, freed from fear, casting off nostalgia, we reject past models. This does not mean denying true experiences but trying to reformulate our understanding of their meaning in such a way that we avoid the faults of the past whilst keeping the insights we cherish. This does not mean new doctrines or creeds but 'a new openness which will allow manifold ways of responding and elucidating that response. These ways may not seem consistent; they may have to co-exist in tension and paradox; but they need not pass judgement on each other.'[54]

So we need to explore next new ways of understanding Jesus and of expressing our knowledge of God.

VI

OF JESUS

What then can we say about Jesus?

The results of modern biblical study show us that we can know for certain very little about Jesus. Although we have criteria for trying to decide which of his teachings are authentic, the accounts of his sayings and actions have come to us from a church which was both selecting and developing the tradition. They were written down by evangelists who were concerned with interpreting their meaning for their contemporary church groups.

The evidence is capable of various interpretations. Jesus has been represented as a prophet, a wandering rabbi, a leader of guerrilla revolution, a prototype for monk and priest. These say more about our needs than about historical truth.

Can we say then that Jesus was in any way a perfect man or an example to us? Such evidence as we have tells us that Jesus was a man of his time, limited by the knowledge and culture available to him. He was not perfect in knowledge or in his interpretation of religion—there were times when he said things which we now regard as mistaken.

Was his behaviour then perfect? The ideas that Jesus was 'good' and 'loving' may be judgements which we read back into the situation without considering the evidence or the implications. The argument goes, God is loving, Jesus is God, therefore Jesus is loving. But if we apply the words 'good' and 'loving' to Jesus we are using the words in unusual ways.

What did Jesus demonstrate of loving? There is no evidence of any family love. He is not known to have married and he quarrelled with his mother and brothers. There is no evidence of the love involved in stable community living. Much of the evidence of his compassion is in situations such as healing miracles which we cannot emulate. There is no evidence to suggest that his death was the result of love for humanity.

There is evidence of love towards friends and the outcasts of society and those who were seeking God. But this is not the whole meaning of the word 'love'.

Was he good? When we ask this question, there is an underlying assumption of the Kantian moral imperative. That is, by 'good' we mean that behaviour which is good at all times and in all places. How much of the behaviour of Jesus is this sort of example? We surely cannot suggest that the ideal behaviour for everyone is to be a celibate, jobless, miracle-worker? Indeed, if we were all celibate and jobless, we would need to work miracles!

It might be more promising to suggest that Jesus' love was towards God and that his goodness was obedience to God's will which he interpreted for his own time and situation as we should do for ours. We must recognise, however, that we can have little knowledge of Jesus' mind or intentions—we may be interpreting beyond the evidence.

A different way of describing the person of Jesus comes from Macquarrie who says that he is definitive 'in the sense that for Christians he defines in normative fashion both the nature of man ... and the nature of God.' 'In Christ there is an entire constellation of qualities which we recognise as constituting the essence of authentic personal being.'[55]

But what is 'authentic personal being' and can one man be a model for it? I would suggest to you that Jesus can only be a model for that element of authenticity which is brought by facing death. He cannot however be a model for the fullness of human life. No one person can represent the authenticity which we find in community, and especially in our closest relationships such as friendship, marriage and parenthood.

More seriously, the use of Jesus as definitive for the nature of man means that a whole half of humanity is left out. Not only are women robbed of the authenticity of their deepest experiences, in particular of the experience of childbirth, but the model of humanity and of God is robbed of the qualities which women have to offer.

Whilst bishops can say, and seriously mean, such things as 'The sexuality of Christ is no accident nor is his masculinity incidental. This is the divine choice,'[56] we are being offered not a definition of humanity but what Daly calls 'incorporation with Yahweh and Son'.[57]

If we take seriously the insight of the priestly writer (*Genesis*, 1:27), 'God created man in his own image; male and female created he them,' then the fullness of both humanity and Godhood is neither masculine nor feminine exclusively but incorporates, and goes beyond, both. For this, Jesus cannot be definitive.

We shall consider God later. But both here and in our discussion of redemption we have seen that Christianity is based on a defective definition of humanity. There is an urgent need for a new definition of humanity based not on patriarchal traditions nor on matriarchal fantasies but on an honest and profound study of what it means to be human, including the experience of women and men as individuals and as a community. The Society of Friends is, I believe, well placed to undertake such a task.

We see, then, that what we can say about the historical Jesus is very limited. Can we even say that he was unique? If we look at him in isolation we can say both that he was unique, but that this is true of every human being, and that he was not unique in the sense that there is nothing in his teachings and actions that has not been seen in some other life. There have been other martyrs, other teachers, others who have forgiven those who harmed them, other workers of miracles, others reported as raised from the dead.

What is unique about Jesus lies not so much in himself as in the community which responded to him. His life and death, the resurrection experience and the impetus to follow him made a 'Christ-event' which is unique.

Macquarrie writes, 'He is unintelligible apart from the whole complex of relationships which bind him to Israel, to the Church, to the entire human race, and it is this vast ongoing movement of spiritual transformation and renewal that has to be borne in mind when we consider the claim made for Christ.'[58]

In speaking about Jesus, therefore, we are speaking not of one man but of a whole complex of response and interpretation based on an historical event, and still going on today. Seen in this way we can speak of the love of Jesus towards outcasts and sinners, of his love and obedience towards God, for we are not speaking historically, but in a way which shows what we find significant. What is important about Jesus is what we respond to in our most profound religious moments.

When we talk of the Christ-event, then, we may find two ways of describing Jesus which are helpful and point a way for further development. The first is the inspired man. That is, Jesus may be seen as one who was fully responsive to the spirit of God and who followed the leadings of that spirit even unto death. He placed his life and talents at God's disposal in such a way that the spirit of God was made manifest more clearly than ever before.

Lampe says, 'It is this Christ-Spirit for which we claim decisiveness; the Spirit disclosed as the inspiration and power of human thought and will and action in Jesus himself and in the whole cluster or body of experience of God which has Jesus as its focus.'[59]

The 'Spirit of Christ' must thus be seen not as a Spirit

emanating from a divine Christ but as that Spirit of God which was in Jesus, to which Jesus responded, and which became manifest in the Christ-event. It is thus equivalent to the Inner Light for it is universally available. However, the teachings and deeds of Jesus as mediated to us provide a guide to its recognition.

The second way of describing Jesus is as the 'bearer of revelation'.[60] Through the response to the spirit seen in his life and death, words and deeds he became the vehicle through which the nature of God was disclosed to us. And this was not the revelation of doctrines or forms of words but the disclosure of a person. 'What is offered to man's apprehension in any specific Revelation is not truth concerning God but the living God himself.'[61]

The extraordinary thing about the Christ-event is that it reveals the redeeming love of God. As Küng describes it,

> He does not demand but gives, does not oppress but raises up, does not wound but heals. He spares those who impugn his holy law and thus attack himself. He forgives instead of condemning, liberates instead of punishing, permits the unrestricted rule of grace instead of law. He is therefore the God who turns, not to the righteous, but to the unrighteous. The God who prefers the sinner, the prodigal, to the one who stayed at home, the tax collector to the Pharisee, the heretics to the orthodox, the prostitutes and adulterers to their judges, the lawbreakers and outlaws to the guardians of the law.[62]

Above all, the revelation of the Christ-event is of the God who takes on the suffering of the world, forgiving, reconciling, calling us through love and weakness, the God who is saviour and salvation; whose love is such that it gives us freedom to mock, deny or kill God; the God who would, who does, die for us and in us in the process of creating us into what we should be, who calls us into that quality of response that Jesus had, to manifest the 'kingdom'.

Two questions remain. First, in being the bearer of revelation is Jesus also the content of that revelation? That is, may we speak of Jesus as divine?

I suggest that the model of the 'bearer of revelation' can be held without there being any logical necessity to maintain the divinity of Jesus. But there are those Friends whose experience of God is so closely bound to Jesus that they will find this conclusion unacceptable. For them it will be necessary to consider what divinity might mean in this context.

The most promising approach is to consider the Christ-event as symbol. On the one hand it could symbolise that the perfection of humanity is incorporation into divinity, 'the coming into one of deity and humanity, of creative Being and creatively being. ... Christ is the first-fruits but the Christian hope is that "in Christ", God will bring all men to God-manhood.'[63] Faith in Jesus thus becomes faith in God's ultimate redeeming purpose, though it is possible to believe in this purpose without faith in Jesus. To see Jesus as the first to reach the human destiny of union with God may permit us to call him divine but this does not justify a theology either of incarnation or of pre-existence.

On the other hand, we can respond to the Christ-event in such a way that we see Jesus as a symbol of God, a concrete example of divine being and action. When we do this, though we make statements focused on Jesus, we are in fact trying to talk about God.

Using this symbol, we can talk about God as helpless and humble, sharing human vulnerability with us. We can see the broken-ness of God, the giving up of power in order to take on pain and mortality; the creativity of love which remakes hope out of despair, promise out of sin; the incarnation of the divine in the human, making all of life sacred; the fusion of holiness with life; the divine self-offering.

Using this symbol we can talk about comfort; about the light that shines in the darkness; about the certainty of love and joy. We can see the presence of God in every aspect of our lives so that whatever our situation it is shared and understood.

Using this symbol, we can, above all, see God in our fellow-humans, and thus be called to service. In every homeless child, every refugee, every criminal or outcast, every worker or preacher, those in authority and those without it, there is a child of God, one who is precious and loved.

The second question is whether this is a complete revelation of God. Is it the only, or the final, revelation? Can we say that 'the only meaning of the word God which is worth discussing is the meaning which Jesus gave it?'[64]

I suggest that our Quaker experience will not allow this. For if we believe that the Inner Light is available to everyone, we must see God's self-disclosure in many events and lives, and a world-wide possibility of interpreting the ways of God. And this is in fact what happens. God is revealed not only in well-known ways, the Exodus, the Exile, through Muhammad, Buddha, Gandhi, Guru Nanak, George Fox, but in countless millions of happenings and people, wherever we have eyes to see.

There will be those who wish to say that the Christ-event is the most significant of these revelations. But they must not forget that a part of that revelation is their own response. They can only say 'This is the revelation in which God is most sig-nificantly disclosed to me' or 'This is the revelation which holds together the worshipping community'. These are judgements of value which cannot be held as absolutely true or as having any validity outside those who make them. We cannot judge God's interactions with others—only marvel at the infinite variety and creativity of the divine spirit.

VIIa

OF REVELATION

In seeing Jesus, or the Christ-event, as the 'bearer of revelation' we have one model of the way in which God is disclosed to us. We shall now consider other ways in which we know of God, and in doing this we shall use the concept of simultaneous models.

All along we have supposed that God wishes to communicate with us, to be in relationship with us and to draw response from us, but that this is done in such a way as to preserve our freedom. God is not limited to one mode of communication and no one mode could lead us to the fullness of knowledge. The ways of God's self-disclosure are potentially infinite. If I may stretch anthromorphic language, I shall call them 'God's models'. By this I do not mean that they are pictures or replicas of God but signs or symbols which lead us to various aspects of God's being. They are like the parables. In the parables of Jesus, the kingdom of God is variously described as being like a farmer, like a seed, like a pearl, like a feast, but none of these is to be taken literally. The parables are of worth only as they call forth response and understanding.

God's models too are not to be taken literally, but seen as an attempt to lead us into deeper relationship. From the Godward side they are the ways of revelation, how God is self-revealed to us. From the side of humanity, they are the ways of experience, how God is met, known, understood and interpreted in human life. Thus revelation and experience are not opposed concepts. They are the same events perceived from different mental stances. 'God's models' therefore can equally be seen as human models which attempt to record and interpret ultimate meaning.

63

I shall consider six models of the way in which God is revealed to us. They are chosen because of their significance in some of the major religious traditions and thus demonstrate in part the universality of revelation. Nevertheless, I recognise that I discuss them from within the Christian tradition and that what I say is coloured by my own culture and presuppositions. The descriptions here need to be rounded out by discussion with those of other traditions. The models are the universe and the natural world; the community; history; the scriptures; worship and the arts; and Jesus.

From our experience of the universe we gain concepts of immensity and infinity. It speaks to us of the greatness of God, of otherness, of transcendence.

> The heavens declare the glory of God and the firmament shows his handywork. (*Psalm*, 19:1.)

> He that makes the Pleiades and Orion and turns the shadow of death into the morning and makes the day dark with night; that calls for the waters of the sea and pours them out upon the face of the earth; the Lord is his name. (*Amos*, 5:8.)

> > The heaven is thy salver, the sun and moon thy lamps,
> > The stars in their paths are thy scattered pearls.
> > The fragrance of sandalwood is thy incense,
> > The wind is thy royal fan and all the flowers thy forest,
> >   Lord of Light.[65]

Norman Pittenger[66] points out that the natural world shows God's boundless creativity—'An aesthetic glory, an imagination, creative dreaming and working,' and through consistency and regularity, that God is faithful, sustaining and preserving though also doing new things.

When we look at the very small, we may see the care lavished on the perfection of tiny creatures. The universe and the world are ordered, yet essentially out of our control.

They draw from us the responses of wonder, awe, even terror. They provide the great metaphors of God as Rock—the eternal and trustworthy—and Light—that by which we see and understand.

The second model, the community, reveals God in a different way. It is here that we learn about relationships, about love and forgiveness, about accepting ourselves and others with all our faults and virtues. Here we see that we cannot stand alone, that we are interdependent. We learn responsibility and we learn to let others be. It is in community that we grow as persons.

As we struggle with the problems of living together in the world we develop understanding of justice, of righteousness, of pity and mercy. We learn of freedom, courage and commitment.

The community mediates to us and teaches us all the qualities we need for relationships with God. We learn what it means to be human and to respond with all the potentialities of humanity.

It is here that we respond by finding some of the personal metaphors for God, the shepherd, seeking out, comforting and leading the flock, and the parent,[67] teaching, feeding, and caring for her children, finding in our relationships and cares signs that point us to God. Yet this is the model, above all, that is available to everyone whether or not they express a belief in God.

Pittenger writes:

> It was William James, I believe, who once remarked that 'God is no gentleman; he doesn't care what you call him.' Sometimes he is called—that is known and served as—love of friend or neighbour. Sometimes he is called justice for the underprivileged. Sometimes he is called truth, such as the scientist seeks to discover. Sometimes he is called beauty, which the artist and poet seek to depict. Sometimes, and

often, he is honesty and responsible service in business and school and industry and in daily contact with others. He may be called 'taking care of little Johnny who is ill' or 'nursing grandmother, who is unable to look out for herself'. My point is that in all activity which is *right* activity, God is present; but he is often present under his incognito and we are not to seek to violate that incognito under those particular circumstances.[68]

Thus, God is present in all human striving, in every act of love and compassion and service.

The third of 'God's models' is history, perhaps particularly significant in Judaism. The art of history is interpretation and it is here in particular that we are faced with the struggle to find purpose and meaning in life, and in finding this purpose we are helped to cope with all that is harsh, horrible and unlovely in human existence.

We can see patterns of significance. We can see how dreadful events are overcome, how there can be reconciliation and healing. And so we are able to look forward with hope and trust. It is in the contemplation of history that God is revealed to us as a deliverer—and as providence.

This is not without its difficulties. We have already realised that the world is ambiguous and that history raises acutely the problem of suffering. But it may show us the power of God. 'I form the light, and create darkness; I make peace, and create evil; I am the Lord that doeth all these things.' (*Isaiah*, 45:7.)

We may see within history a pattern of 'death and resurrection'; of slavery followed by exodus, of exile followed by restoration, of holocaust by renewal, of persecution by strengthening. None of this is to deny the horrors of human history or to excuse the cruelties men have practised. But yet it gives us faith that God can never be defeated. It calls from us the response of

trust; that trust which ceases to find security in worldly possessions and positions and places its confidence in the only
certainty and hope; that trust which declares that, 'they that sow
in tears shall reap in joy. Though he goes forth on his way
weeping, bearing the seed; he shall come again with joy, bringing
his sheaves with him.' (*Psalm*, 126: 5-6.)

In suggesting scriptures as a fourth model, I am using the
term widely to cover the sacred and significant writings of all
faiths. As George Fox wrote, 'The spirit that gave forth the
Scriptures teacheth us ... how to read them with understanding
and how to walk before God and man.'[69]

In no sense are the Christian scriptures to be taken as literally
true or as binding. We are subject to the results of Biblical study.
Muslims however regard the Koran as binding, though they do
discuss how to interpret it.

This is what Leo Baeck, a Jew, writes of the Torah, oral and
written.

> It is a book composed and written down, and it is at the
> same time a movement, awakened and renewing itself from
> within. It has its word with which it begins and its word with
> which it ends. But in reality it never ceases and never ends;
> ever again it commences and continues. Its word seems to
> be a word that was spoken once, but it is in reality a task
> that starts itself again and again. He who believes that he
> carries it in his hand does not have it, but he who is driven
> by it, to him has it come.[70]

In the long process of the relationship of God and humanity,
of the divine revelation and the human interpretation, some
moments, events and insights have been seen as having outstanding significance. And, of these, some have been crystal-
lised in writing and preserved. We are not excused from using

67

our judgement for some of the gems may be false, some worthless.

But the value of the scriptures is that they link us to the long chain of human discoveries and responses; to Abraham discovering other ways of trust than human sacrifice (*Genesis*, 22), to Elijah hearing the still small voice (*I Kings*, 19:12), to Micaiah standing up to two kings and four hundred official yes-men to proclaim God's will (*I Kings*, 22). They put us into contact with the triumph of Miriam (*Exodus*, 15: 20-21) and Deborah (*Judges*, 5), the grief and joy of Hannah (*I Samuel*, 1 and 2), the faithfulness of Ruth. As we share the important moments of their lives, the dimensions of our experience are opened up. We learn from their discoveries and mistakes and we join in the search for permanent values, for 'the true religion which doth never change,'[71] and for the spirit from whom they come. We are the more assured of that spirit constantly at work and of the variety of ways in which the divine is known.

The scriptures lead us from and through themselves to the one who inspires and guides human insights. As one of the Hindu scriptures says, 'Of what use is the Rig Veda to one who does not know the Spirit from whom the Rig Vida comes, and in whom all things abide. For only those who have found him have found peace.'[72]

The fifth of God's models is worship. For us this is in silence with a minimum of ritual; but worship can be dramatic, colourful, full of symbols, adorned with music and art and light and movement.

There is the sombre beauty and controlled emotion of a requiem sung in a great cathedral; the thrilling moment in a synagogue when the ark is opened and the scroll of the law brought out, the great symbol of a long relationship between God and a people. There is the Sikh temple where colour and decoration and hospitality contribute to a feeling of being at home in the heart of a community; there is the steady and dutiful devotion in the mosque.

And springing out of this the great arts of drama, music, painting, sculpture, ceramics, calligraphy which have partly gone their own independent way.

What worship and its attendant arts does is to represent to us the transcendent breaking into our lives. Whatever the means by which the divine reaches us, whether silence, beauty, devotion, ritual, it makes claims upon us, not only on our time and possessions, but on our lives. It sets out to evoke response, and however this response is expressed, its basis is a turning to God of the individual and the worshipping community, a refreshment of spirit, a recreation of vision and purpose. At the same time worship, by its patterns, controls and directs this response, using the tradition of the community as a guide to see that we do not over-reach ourselves or turn in wrong directions.

Of course, worship runs the danger of becoming empty ritual, rules to be obeyed and actions to be performed whose meaning has been lost. What is of value is not the form itself but the way in which it discloses God to us and enables us to respond. It can evoke contrition, devotion, praise and joy, and bring us closer to God and each other.

The last model to discuss is Jesus. And here we see the value of considering what the model discloses of God rather than what it is in itself. For we may not reach any degree of agreement over who Jesus is. For some he will always be 'the centre of our faith, the ground of our assurance that we really know the character of God'.[73] For others he will never be more than an outstanding leader and teacher. But if we ask the right question, this disagreement becomes irrelevant. Though our beliefs will be important to each of us as individuals, to us as a Society it does not matter whether we regard Jesus as God or man. What does matter, what this model discloses to us, is the way in which God works.

It reveals God as reaching out to humanity, as working 'to seek and to save the lost'. It reveals the unexpected qualities of God, the upsetting of human values and order. The involvement of God with the criminal, the suffering, the oppressed, with all that is unlovely in human life, is a sure ground of hope, a strong basis for community and an invitation to abandon certainty and live with risk.

Thus we may answer the question 'Are Quakers Christian?' by saying that it does not matter. What matters to Quakers is not the label by which we are called or call ourselves, but the life. The abandonment of self to God means also the abandonment of labels, of doctrines, of cherished ways of expressing the truth. It means the willingness to follow the spirit wherever it leads, and there is no guarantee that this is to Christianity or to any 'happy ending' except the love, peace and unity of God.

Like the sword which Fox told Penn to wear as long as he could, we take our religion and beliefs as far as we can, we take our morality and notions of goodness as far as we can, we take our ideas of truth as far as we can. All these are good. But they are not what we seek. In the end, we place them into the hands of God, in trust, to make or break, to crown or destroy, for they are nothing in themselves, but God is all in all.

VIIb

OF FAITH

We have explored six of the models through which God is disclosed to us. There are other models, as many perhaps as there are individuals to see, but these are public models in the sense that they are available to all and that most feature in some at least of the world's major religions.[74]

Each model has its dangers. In the first three, there are the dangers of reaching facile and simplistic conclusions, which ignore ambiguity and cruelty, and assume that 'all is for the best in the best of all possible worlds', without demanding of God the righteousness and integrity we ask of ourselves. In the latter three, the dangers are of literalism leading to emptiness without real life and response. These dangers may be summed up as a concentration on the model rather than on what it reveals of God or the response it evokes. As George Herbert wrote:

A man that looks on glass,
On it may stay his eye,
Or if he pleases through it pass
And then the heavens espy.

These models are like the glass. If we look at them for too long we may lose sight of what lies beyond. Their purpose is to be signs of transcendence, models of the divine, to lead us into the light and call forth love of God and our neighbour in the unity of the spirit.

These models may be held simultaneously, but it is not intended that any one of them should be regarded as essential. God is revealed to individuals through models suited to their temperaments and abilities; to communities through models suited to their culture. Nor will the interpretation of these models

71

always be the same. Each one is only a guide to the truth that is greater than them all yet accessible in the nearest and simplest way.

This concept of simultaneous models all of which may disclose God has immense and valuable consequences.

Firstly, for individuals it allows both for personal response and for change and development. As our experience widens we are brought closer to aspects of God which we did not understand before. But we are compelled to respect the experience and response of others. If there is no one model of the truth and if no model is essential then there is no basis for authoritarianism or heresy-hunts. Our own vision is widened by the vision of others. Thus, this concept is compatible with the principles of Quakerism.

Secondly, it helps us to answer the Quaker problem of the tension between Christ-centredness and universalism. We may see these as two emphases, two ways out of many in which God is disclosed. Both are significant to Quakerism, but neither is the whole truth. The truth of God is greater than both of these models, and this principle is maintained by the maintenance of the tension which comes from holding both simultaneously.

It is a difficult task, but one which is essential to Quakerism if we are to remain 'the people that must stand in the gap' (William Penn).

If we can maintain this tension, then the concept of simultaneous models has further consequences. It allows us to find a basis on which we may move towards unity with the Christian churches, neither disowning our own insights nor disparaging theirs. But at the same time it gives us a basis for extending far beyond Quakerism and Christianity and into the whole world of religions.

Each faith can be seen as receiving disclosures of ultimate truth and responding to that truth in ways of life. Each faith is at

72

its worst where it concentrates on exclusive interpretation of a model at the expense of love and unity; at its best when it goes beyond to the universal which is disclosed to all.

Thus we have a theological basis for being able to be both Christian (or any other faith) and universalist; committed to the ways in which God is disclosed to us and open to all other divine disclosure. We have a way of sharing common human experience and enjoying the different expressions of that experience. We have a way of knowing truth whilst recognising other aspects of the same truth. We have a way in which loyalty to the spirit we feel can lead to unity and fellowship with all.

We may rejoice with their joys, grieve with their sorrows, sympathise with their struggles and praise their successes, knowing that the same spirit is at work amongst them, the same reconciling purpose and that their ultimate end is the same.

Further, we have a basis for a new form of 'evangelism', not one of proclaiming but of inquiring. For this 'gospel' requires that we seek truth and that our words should thus be 'What canst thou say? How is God known to you? What can you tell us of the ultimate purpose as it is disclosed in your life and situation?'

As we learn so we may change. But there is no need to fear. Whatever our outward circumstances, if we truly seek God, we shall be found and safely held.

Finally, the concept of simultaneous models of God's disclosure places the emphasis of our theology where it should most properly lie, that is, not on the models themselves but on the God who is revealed. So that in the end we must consider how we may speak of God.

VIII

IN THE END, GOD

*Scrutator enim majestatis opprimatur a gloria.**

—Martin Luther

Finally, we turn to the proper task of theology, which is to talk of God. This is an urgent and important matter, for if the doctrine of the Trinity is unsatisfactory, there is a gaping hole in our thinking.

The problem which that doctrine set out to resolve is still with us, and that is the problem of reconciling two ways of thought, the Jewish tradition which saw God as active and involved in events, and the Greek metaphysical tradition which paid what Whitehead called 'metaphysical compliments' attributing to God all perfections in such a way that there was no possibility of God being involved in time and change. The tension between these two ways is still with us.

In particular there are the problems of how we can speak of God as eternal, that is outside time, and yet active in history; how can we say that God is changeless and yet responds to us in loving and suffering with us; how can we express the perfection of God which must be beyond our comprehension and yet speak of God's personality or relationship to us in a personal way.[75]

For if we attempt to say that all these are true are we not contradicting ourselves?

It is here that the concept of simultaneous models helps us too, for it helps us to make a very careful distinction between God, and the ways in which we express our differing experiences of the divine. Thus the tension, or paradox or contradic-

* 'For the searcher-out of God's greatness is overwhelmed by glory'.

tion is not to be placed in the character or nature of God, but in the need to use many models in order to express truth as fully as possible.

Therefore what we say is provisional, symbolic and metaphorical. So that when we speak of God in a personal way we do not mean that God is a person, only that personal language is the best we have to express an inexpressible relation. When we speak of God as changeless we are using by analogy a word for which we have no referent. Everything that we know changes, living things grow and die, the rocks are formed and ground to sand, the sun cools. What we mean by the 'metaphysical compliment' of changeless is that God is utterly reliable and trustworthy. And when we speak of God as eternal we mean that the same ultimate purpose is to be discerned in past, present and future.

If we look at the ways in which we speak of God we can see three ways,[76] modelled on language. We speak of God as a noun, an adjective and a verb. No one of these ways is in itself adequate and each has its faults and difficulties. Nor are all three together sufficient. But they provide different insights and mutual criticism, and the tension and paradox within which a glimpse of the greater truth might lie.

To conclude, then, let us consider in turn each of these models of God.

The first and traditional use of the word 'God' is as a noun. It emphasises above all God's transcendence and difference from us. This is the creator God of whom we use such words as majesty, power, glory, eternal, infinite, ineffable; of whom the psalmist wrote,

> O Lord my God, thou art very great; thou art clothed with
> honour and majesty.
> Who coverest thyself with light as with a garment; who

stretchest out the heavens like a curtain:
Who layeth the beams of his chambers in the waters;
Who maketh the clouds his chariot; who walketh upon the
wings of the wind;
Who laid the foundations of the earth, that it should not be
moved for ever. (*Psalm*, 104: 1-3, 5.)

For this God we use metaphors such as king, judge, father.
This model serves to evoke and express responses of awe,
wonder, humility, terror. This is the God who calls forth
worship. But there are difficulties in this model of God.

The first is that it distances and objectifies God—it leads to
philosophical concepts like the 'Unmoved Mover'. There is a
danger of God being seen as remote, abstract and unconcerned.
It led, in the past, to the need to posit mediators so that God
could interact with mankind, and hence the development of the
concepts of the Shekinah, Wisdom, the Logos, the Son. There is
a danger, too, that the God of metaphysics may be substituted
for the God of religion—as happens in those philosophical argu-
ments which try to prove the existence of God—if they succeed
at all it is in proving the existence of a being bearing no resem-
blance to any God who is worshipped.

The second difficulty is in finding a pronoun. I have been
carefully avoiding 'he' as it suggests that God is masculine, but
'she' is equally inaccurate, and 'it' does not do justice to the need
for personal language.[77] Today more than ever we see that the
image of a masculine God is both the creation and the ideo-
logical support of a patriarchal society and we must deny this
perversion of the name of God—though it is hard to break old
habits. Fortunately, there is a pronoun available which is both
sexless and personal; perhaps we may follow Buber in using
'Thou'.

A third difficulty is that this is the model of God which is most misunderstood and abused. God is used to support power and authoritarianism; it is the name in which wars are fought and persecutions carried out. Can we use a word that is so defiled?

Buber answered this,

> Yes, it is the most heavy-laden of all human words. None has become so soiled, so mutilated. Just for this reason I may not abandon it. Generations of men have laid the burden of their anxious lives upon this word and weighed it to the ground; it lies in the dust and bears their whole burden. . . . Where might I find a word like to describe the highest! If I took the purest, most sparkling concept from the inner treasure-chamber of the philosophers, I could only capture thereby an unbinding product of thought. I could not capture the presence of Him whom generations of men have honoured and degraded with their awesome living and dying. I do indeed mean Him whom the hell-tormented and heaven-storming generations of men mean. . . . But when all madness and delusion fall to dust, when they stand over against Him in the loneliest darkness and no longer say 'He, He' but rather sigh 'Thou', shout 'Thou', all of them the one word, and when they add 'God', is it not the real God whom they all implore, the One Living God, the God of the children of man? . . . And just for this reason is not the word 'God', the word of appeal, the word which has become a *name*, consecrated in all human tongues for all time?[78]

God as a noun then is the word of appeal, the word of mystery and the word of otherness. But there are dangers in its use which need to be corrected against the other two models.

The second model that we use is of God as adjective—the divine. This is the immanent aspect of God, the divine to be found in all creation and in all people. Using this model we see the whole world as in God's gracious presence and therefore holy and sacramental, drawing from us a response of reverence and care.

In the Psalms we find,

> Whither shall I go from thy spirit? or whither shall I flee from thy presence?
>
> If I ascend up into heaven, thou art there; if I make my bed in Sheol, behold, thou art there.
>
> If I take the wings of the morning, and dwell in the uttermost parts of the sea;
>
> Even there shall thy hand lead me, and thy right hand shall hold me.
>
> If I say, Surely the darkness shall overwhelm me, and the light about me shall be night;
>
> Even the darkness hideth not from thee; but the night shineth as the day; the darkness and the light are both alike to thee. (*Psalm*, 139: 7-12.)

The divine is also seen in people, in all people as they respond to life with love and trust and in the growth towards the fullness of humanity. Some see it most in Jesus but it is in every act of self-sacrifice and consideration, in courage and commitment, in forgiveness and healing, in reconciliation and mercy, in the weakness of the weak and the strength of the strong. It is the spirit behind, 'Inasmuch as ye did it unto one of these my brethren, even these least, ye did it unto me.' (*Matthew*, 25:40.)

This divine challenges us to suspend judgement, to care about and respect others. This is the divine tenderness, the love and upholding, closer than heartbeats, nearer than breathing, evoking in us responsibility and gentleness and compassion.

But this model too is inadequate. First it is too easy for it to slip into pantheism, from seeing the divine in all things to seeing all things as divine. It seems to limit God to the created order and by itself has no place for God's difference from creation.

Secondly, in seeing the divine within all people we have not sufficiently allowed for the need for response. God is present to us not as ourselves but as mystery, as other, as the light that enlightens, that inspires action, vision, and authentic being.

Thirdly, this model poses acutely the problem of evil, both of moral evil and physical suffering without having in itself any resources to solve the problem.

So we need both of these models to balance each other, the outer and the inner, the transcendent and the immanent, the terror and the tenderness, the glory and the vision. But even this is not sufficient fully to describe our experience of God. For this we need to add the third model, God as verb.[79]

One verb that is frequently used of God is Being, sometimes extended by Becoming. This use has difficulties if we remain in the philosophical mode of thinking. There are not only the speculative problems such as abstraction, and objectification, but also this use is commonly associated with existentialist philosophy which defines authentic existence by reference to the knowledge of death and mortality, and it is difficult to see how this sort of being could be posited of God.

I believe that we must be exceedingly cautious before we dare to speculate on the Being of God for this above all will exceed our capacities.

However we may perhaps use this model not in a rational but in a mystical way, rather as Penington when he speaks of 'the true peace, the true righteousness, the true holiness, the true rest of the soul, the everlasting habitation which the redeemed dwell in.'[80]

Further, to speak of God as Being may well be a model through which we can reach fellowship with those who practise the meditative and contemplative aspects of religions such as Hinduism and Buddhism (perhaps especially with those

Theravada Buddhists whose belief includes no God). I would not therefore exclude this model.

However it is more true to our Quaker experience to speak of God in terms of transitive verbs and verbs of action, as a dynamic spirit acting towards us. This point may be seen in the description from Fox's journal where the love of God is a strengthening power.

> And as I walked towards the gaol, the word of the Lord came to me saying, 'My love was always to thee and thou art in my love'. And I was ravished with the sense of the love of God and greatly strengthened in my inward man. But when I came into the gaol, where those prisoners were, a great power of darkness struck at me, and I sat still, having my spirit gathered into the love of God.[81]

This is the God who is at work in the world, in history, and in every human being, initiating and sustaining the cosmic drama, creating and saving. This is the activity discovered at the Exodus, delivering slaves from bondage, leading, helping, feeding, healing, demanding. Hosea[82] spoke of this in terms of a parent, feeding a baby, teaching it to walk and talk, holding it up to a cheek, and in great conflict of mind over its waywardness.

This is the divine tension of loving judging, judging loving, feeling anger and compassion, grief and joy.

This God is utterly to be trusted, yet totally unexpected, surprising us with providential grace, teasing us with delightful jokes, opening up the future to possibility, including us in the transcendental laughter. This God trusts us, accepting us as we are whilst calling us to be better; offering us the spirit of love and peace but never compelling us; seeming at times to be absent to increase our knowledge of our own capacities.

This God gives and gives again, pitying, sorrowing, seeking, reconciling, strengthening, mourning, blessing. This is the passionate God to whom we respond with trust and hope, laughter and tears, and willing hearts, alone but also in community.

This model too is inadequate by itself. It involves God too much in our interpretations of events and needs to be balanced by rational thought and contemplation. And though it proposes a solution to the problem of suffering by seeing it as involved in the divine activity and shared with God, we are still faced with the problem of human suffering, and indeed human prosperity, when these do not seem to be ways of spiritual progress. It needs to be balanced by the sense of mystery.

It also risks our misunderstanding of God because all that we say of divine action is by analogy from humanity and this is plainly inadequate.

We have considered three models of God—the noun, the adjective and the verb. If you have recognised any truth in them, the truth was not in the words which are mere symbols but in the knowledge in your own hearts, where the one truth resides and is not, is known and not known, speaks and waits.

We must use all these ways to speak of God for none will do of itself. Nor are all adequate together. But we may hope to be brought closer to the truth in holding the tension of simultaneous models, the transcendent, the immanent and the active; the greatness and the closeness, the beyond and the within, the dynamic and the resting.

But in the end, this is the truth not of words but of response, of the living relationship of worship, love, trust and hope, of God in us and we in God, caught up out of self and out of time into the foreshadowing of what shall be and ever is. We are called to turn to that tenderest compassion, that inexpressible glory, that most profound humility, that deepest friendship, that truest vision, to the God who meets us, whom we know, in the silence, waiting.

REFERENCES AND NOTES

1 Rachel H. King, *George Fox and the Light Within*. Philadelphia: Friends Book Store, 1940. *Out of print*.

2 George Fox, *Journal* ed. by J. L. Nickalls. London Yearly Meeting, 1952, rptd. 1975, pp. 27-8.

3 The quotations from George Fox's Epistles are taken from the original 1698 edition, *A collection of many select and Christian principles*. More readily available is a recently published selection, *No more but my love: letters of George Fox, Quaker* selected and edited by Cecil Sharman (Quaker Home Service, 1980). However, not all the epistles quoted here appear in this selection.

4 George Fox, Epistle 388 (1683). Epistle 366 (1682) speaks of 'the spirit of God both in the Turks and the Moors' and Epistle 379 (1682) 'answer the light and truth and spirit of God in the Indians their Kings and people'.

5 Isaac Penington, 'Concerning the Light' in *The Works*, London, 1681, part 2, p. 335.

6 Fox's *Journal, op. cit.*, p. 668. See also Epistles 248, 291, 301, 313, 320, 321, 360 and passim. Some to be found in Sharman, *op. cit.*

7 William Penn, 'A key opening the way to every capacity' (1692) in *The Works*, London, 1726, vol. 2, p. 781.

8 King, *op. cit.*, p. 42.

9 See George Fox's Epistle 249 for the splendid, 'What! are all true Christians priests? Yes, what are women priests? Yes, women priests'.

10 David E. Jenkins, *The contradiction of Christianity*. SCM, 1976, p. 83.

11 King, *op. cit.*, p. 165, 'Fox identifies the light with the pre-existent Christ and he identifies the pre-existent Christ with the historical Jesus. Jesus did not have a human nature ... (he) inclines to Apollinarianism with a tendency to Sabellianism'.

12 King, *ibid.*, p. 161.

13 Henry Cadbury, *Quakerism and early Christianity* (Swarthmore Lecture, 1957). Allen & Unwin, 1957, p. 48, see also p. 25ff.

14 John Macmurray, *The search for reality in religion* (Swarthmore Lecture, 1965). Friends Home Service Committee, 1965, rptd. 1969, pp. 72-3.

15 I would suggest that the destruction of the Jews in Europe is one of the most significant theological events of the twentieth century.

[16] Isaac Penington, 'The Jew outward: being a glass for the professors of this age' in *The works*, London: 1681, part 1, p. 100.

[17] George Fox, Epistle 47 (1653).

[18] Ian Barbour, *Myths, models and paradigms*. SCM, 1974, p. 136.

[19] I am here freely adapting from the translation by R. C. Zaehner in *Teachings of the Magi: a compendium of Zoroastrian beliefs*. Sheldon Press, 1975.

[20] Barbour, *op. cit.*, p. 53.

[21] In *Early Quaker writings 1650-1700* ed. by Hugh Barbour and Arthur Roberts. Norfolk Press, 1973, p. 382.

[22] William Penn, 'One project for the good of England' (1679) in Barbour and Roberts, *op. cit.*, p. 446.

[23] Richard Baxter, 'One sheet against the Quakers' (1657) in Barbour and Roberts, *op. cit.*, p. 295.

[24] In science the term 'complementary models' is used for two different ways of explaining the same phenomena which are mutually exclusive. See Ian Barbour, *op. cit.*, pp. 71 and 91. Because the models which I use are not necessarily mutually exclusive, I shall use the term 'simultaneous' models for models which cannot in themselves give adequate descriptions and so need to be held in conjunction with other models which may or may not exclude or contradict them.

[25] In a talk to the William Temple Association, October 1978.

[26] This is not, however, to make any political comment on the present State of Israel and its relationships with the Palestinian Arabs.

[27] See for example, *Hosea*, 2:14-20 and 11:1-4; *Psalm* 47; *Ezekiel*, 34:11-16; *Isaiah*, 40:11.

[28] See for example, *Isaiah*, 45: 5-7.

[29] Georg Fohrer, *Introduction to the Old Testament*, trns. by D. Green. SPCK, 1976, p. 383.

[30] As, of course, George Fox believed.

[31] As the day began at sunset on Thursday, evening and night were part of the day of the crucifixion.

[32] Augustine of Hippo in 'Ad Simplicianum', 1, 16.

[33] King, *op. cit.*, p. 41.

[34] Edward Grubb, *Authority and the Light Within*. London: James Clarke, 1908, p. 99.

[35] See, for example, *Pygmalion in the classroom* by Robert Rosenthal and Lenore Jacobson. Eastbourne, Sussex: Holt-Saunders, 1968.

[36] 'You are the devil's gateway ... how easily you destroyed man ... the image of God. Because of the death which you brought upon us, even the Son of God had to die' from *De. Cult. Fem.*, 1.1. See further *Beyond God the father: toward a philosophy of women's liberation* by Mary Daly (Beacon Press, 1977, esp. chapter 2) and *The paradise papers* by Merlin Stone (Virago, 1976, esp. chapters 10 and 11).

[37] See *Isaiah*, 1:10-17; *Amos*, 5:21-25; *Micah*, 6:6-8.

[38] The traditional theories are discussed in chapter 4 of *The remaking of Christian doctrine* by Maurice Wiles (SCM, 1975) and in chapter 21 of *Doctrines of the Creed* by Oliver Quick (Nisbet, 1938).

[39] See, for example, the discussion in *Evil and the God of Love* by John Hick (*paper*, Fontana, 1968 or *cloth* Macmillan, 2nd edn., 1977).

[40] Leonard Hodgson, *For faith and freedom*. London: SCM, 1968, quoted by Hick, *op. cit.*

[41] Geoffrey Lampe, *God as spirit* (Bampton Lecture 1976). Oxford U.P., 1977, p. 17.

[42] John Macquarrie, *Principles of Christian theology*. SCM, rev. edn., 1977.

[43] Hick, *op. cit.*, p. 378ff. Also William Temple quoted in *Our Knowledge of God* by John Baillie. Oxford U.P., 1963, pp. 97-8.

[44] Robert Barclay, *Apology*, propositions 5 and 6.

[45] See the discussions on Forgiveness and Punishment in *God was in Christ* by D. M. Baillie (Faber, 1956, p. 167). Also the discussion on Forgiveness in chapter 1 of *Freedom, Suffering and Love* by Andrew Elphinstone (SCM, 1976).

[46] Recently, for example, *The myth of God incarnate* ed. by John Hick (SCM, 1977) and *The debate about Christ* by Don Cupitt (SCM, 1979).

[47] Hans Lietzmann, *A history of the early church* (4 vols). Lutterworth Press, vol. 3, p. 123.

[48] Ammianus Marcellinus, *Works*, 22, 5, 4.

[49] See the discussion by Zenor in *Concise encyclopaedia of living faiths* by R. C. Zaehner. Hutchinson, 1977.

[50] *Myth of God incarnate, op. cit.*, p. 180.

[51] Lietzmann, *op. cit.*, vol. 4, p. 49.

[52] Gerald Hibbert, *Inner light and modern thought* (Swarthmore Lecture, 1924). London: Swarthmore Press, 1924, p. 59.

[53] John Macmurray, *Ye are my friends* and *To save from fear*. Quaker Home Service, rpt. 1979, pp. 7-8.

[54] Frances Young in *The myth of God incarnate, op. cit.*, p. 38.

[55] Macquarrie, *op. cit.*, pp. 303-5.

[56] A. L. Meyers quoted by Stone, *op. cit.*, p. 254.

[57] Daly, *op. cit.*, p. 184.

[58] Macquarrie, *op. cit.*, p. 304.

[59] Lampe, *op. cit.*, p. 113. The whole chapter on Jesus and the Christ event sets out this model.

[60] I owe this to Macquarrie, *op. cit.*, p. 7.

[61] William Temple quoted in *Our knowledge of God, op. cit.*, p. 36.

[62] Hans Küng, *On being a Christian*, trns. by E. Quinn. Collins, 1977, pp. 312-3.

[63] Macquarrie, *op. cit.*

[64] Maurice Creasey, *Bearings or Friends and the new reformation* (Swarthmore Lecture, 1969). Friends Home Service Committee, 1969, p. 69.

[65] Adi Granth quoted in *Man's religious quest* ed. by Whitfield Foy. Croom Helm, 1977, pp. 275-6.

[66] Norman Pittenger, *God's way with men*. Hodder, 1969, pp. 46-7.

[67] For example, *Ezekiel*, 34:11-16; *Isaiah*, 40:11; *Psalm* 23; *Hosea*, 11:1-4; *Isaiah*, 49:14-16.

[68] Pittenger, *op. cit.*, pp. 81-2.

[69] George Fox, Epistle 171 (1659).

[70] Leo Baeck, *This people Israel*. W. H. Allen, 1965, pp. 199-200.

[71] George Fox, Epistle 171 (1659).

[72] From *The Upanisheds*, trns. from the Sanskrit with an Introduction by Juan Mascaro. Penguin Classics, 1965, part 4, p. 91.

[73] Edward Grubb, *op. cit.*, p. 136.

[74] I recognise that there is a difficulty with Theravada Buddhism which does not talk in terms of God. Nevertheless, the means to Nirvana is disclosed through models such as Scriptures, the community, and an individual, the Buddha.

[75] These problems are discussed in, for example, *Concepts of Deity* by H. P. Owen (Macmillan, 1971); *The Doctrine of God* by R. G. Smith (Collins, 1970); *Thinking about God* by J. Macquarrie (SCM, 1975).

[76] Ian Barbour, *op. cit.*, pp. 155ff, suggests four different models.

[77] See also Hans Küng, *op. cit.*, p. 130.

[78] Martin Buber, *Eclipse of God*, trns. R. G. Smith. Gollancz, 1953, pp. 16ff.
[79] I owe this concept to Daly, *op. cit.*, but interpret it differently from her.
[80] Isaac Penington, 'Account of his spiritual travel' in Barbour and Roberts, *op. cit.*, p. 234.
[81] Fox's *Journal*, *op. cit.*, p. 46.
[82] *Hosea*, 11:1-4 and 8-9.

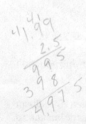